MY BL

Volume 1: My childhood to my young adult years

<u>Chapter One</u>

"Mama, please, I didn't do it. Honestly! They're getting me in trouble for nothing. Mama, why do you hate me?"

My nightmare of a life began at a young age. I can still remember when I was nine years old. My mother, Joyce Brown, was an attractive, shapely woman, with coal-black hair. She always treated me like I was the black sheep of the family by giving special privileges to my twin sister,

Lenise, and my baby brother, Anthony. Lenise

was cute, with a dark complexion and long

hair. In some ways, she had a good heart, but was

often a spoiled manipulator. Anthony was tall,

also with a dark complexion, and was a rude,

spoiled Mama's boy. But when it came to me, it

seemed that I was invisible to Mama—except

when I got into trouble, which was often. There

were times when my brother and sister would wait

until our mother left home before taking food from

the pantry. They would then eat the snacks in

various rooms of the house, such as the bedroom,

the bathroom and the den area. Although they

knew that our mother never allowed us to eat

anywhere except the dining room, Lenise and Anthony would leave the wrappings from their snacks under the couch or under their beds. "Who did this?" This is the question our mother would always ask after coming home and finding the house in a complete mess. Knowing that Mama favored them over me, they would always say, "Denise ate the food and left the wrappings on the floor. We told her not to do it." She never questioned them, and her devilish eyes told me what was about to happen next. "Rochelle Denise Vaughn, get over here!" Going to her closet, mother retrieved her extension cord and begin beating me. A feeling of hate toward her started to overwhelm me, even as I begged her to stop.

"Mama, please, I didn't do it. Honestly! They're getting me in trouble for nothing. Mama, why do you hate me? I never touched anything without your permission." It was useless to try to give my mother an explanation; it actually made her behavior toward me even worse. She would spank me even more, and would then make me stay up all night cleaning up the messes my siblings had made. When I finally finished cleaning, I had to stand in the corner with one leg up in the air as further punishment. If I couldn't keep my leg up, my mother would beat me again. This would continue until 4:00 a.m., when my mother would finally send me to bed. I always hoped that someone would knock on the door and realize my mother was hurting me from the screams, the welts, and the bruises she was often leaving on me. These restless nights meant I was extremely tired in class the next day, due to getting up to go to school at 6:00 a.m. If my teacher told my mother I had fallen asleep during class, my mother would make me sit outside all night on the porch while my brother and sister ate, bathed, and went to bed. My mother would always tell me the same thing while I was waiting for her to finally send me to bed. "You better not tell the school shit, or I'm going to beat your ass some more. Now get your bitch ass on." The next morning, I would be late for school again, because I would have to wash the dishes that they had left in the sink. I also had to make their beds, which made me feel more like the maid in the family than a sister. Cinderella had it easy!

As time went on, things around the house never got any better, only worse. My twin sister and I would stay at my Auntie Velma's house when our mother needed a babysitter. Auntie Velma, an older lady with beautiful hair, was full of wisdom and compassion, providing help and a place to live for many family members who came to her. The house was full of grown children who were either homeless or who had no parents available to raise them. This was due to their parents being incarcerated from drug arrests. These incarcerated parents led these children down the wrong path of committing burglaries, or even capital murder, resulting in the parents often never being able to reclaim their kids if they were released. One evening, Lenise and I spent the night at my Auntie Velma's house. She always arranged the room assignments for everyone, and on this very night I slept in the middle room of the house. I don't know if she thought I was going to try to sneak out or wander through the house at a weird hour of the night. Perhaps she thought there was a possibility of someone clsc cntering my room. Not only did this make Auntie Velma oblivious to anything going on in the house, but that night became one of the worst nights of many during this season of my young life.

Chapter Two

"Take your clothes off. I have a gun," he

whispered.

It was around 2:15 a.m. when I woke up and realized that someone else was in my bed. The room was extremely dark, and I absolutely could not identify who it was. I was 10 years old, and a male voice was telling me to be quiet, or he would hurt me. With his hand over my mouth, I began to cry a little. My crying didn't help, because the next sentence I heard was, "Shut up. I mean it, or you will die right here." My nightmare was just beginning.

I didn't understand what was going on, but I realized that if I didn't do what he demanded, he might murder me. After I had taken all my clothes off, he tied my hands to the bed. At this point I could see a little bit of his head. He put his face between my legs, and began to do something strange down there. Keeping his hand over my mouth, he continued for a long time. After a while, he tried to put his privates in my vagina, and I began to cry. I was afraid, needed help, and wanted to get away from this man as fast as I could. Later, he entered me, and it hurt badly. He was very careful to not leave any sperm in me. It seemed like he raped me all night long. Wiping me up when he finished, I could finally see his face, and I was shocked to see the face of my first cousin, Leon.

He said, "You better not tell anyone. You hear me?" I couldn't help, but cry again at this point. I just nodded, and said that I wouldn't ever tell anyone. I was extremely afraid of my cousin Leon. Not only was he a drug dealer, but he was also a drug user. He finally left my bedroom and lay down on the living room couch as if he'd done nothing wrong. My Auntie Velma got up the next morning, came into my room, and asked me to get ready. This meant taking a bath before eating breakfast. Since there were so many people in the house, she always made the children bathe first.

When I got up from the bed, I saw that I was bleeding everywhere. "Auntie Velma, can you come help me?" I didn't understand what was happening to me. Auntie Velma exclaimed, "Girl, I guess you're starting your cycle early. Baby, let's get you fixed up." I wanted so badly to tell her that the man she had raised was running around sleeping with children, but his threats continued to play in my mind. Thus, I never opened my mouth to tell anyone, because I was fearful of what he might do to, and not just to me. He could possibly harm my twin sister, or even the whole family. Leon was a very disturbed person, and honestly, I don't think anyone knew how to relate to him. He had been locked up for murder before, but my auntie still allowed him to live in her home when he was on parole. Leon was her son, and no matter what he did, she was going to help him. I wasn't sure to what extent that would have continued if I had shared his raping of me with her. I didn't even tell my mother, because she would accuse me of causing more problems.

However, my oldest sister, Marcy, finally contacted our mother, who had gone out of town with some guy, and they had just returned. Marcy was extremely upset about us staying at Auntie Velma's house. She wanted to know why we were there, and why Mama hadn't been over to see us.

Marcy wasn't sure if our mother had visited us, or not; she just truly felt that our mother should have had us with her. Lenise and I, with my mother's approval, began to stay with Marcy for a few months, until Joyce finally found another place to live. Anthony had been residing with his father, and then returned home to our mother at the same time that Lenise and I were returned. Finally, all three us were back at home.

About six months later, we went back into the normal, discouraging routine of me doing everything around the house. As usual, my siblings lay around the house, doing nothing. This continued for three years.

I was now 13 years of age, and I started questioning myself. Why is it okay to be mistreated? I could never come up with a satisfactory answer. Our mother had begun doing some additional janitorial work for a cleaning company at night. She felt that since I was 13 years old, I needed a job to help her take care of my siblings, so I began to work. Mama would often take my paycheck and pay her bills with it. I honestly didn't mind helping to support my siblings. After a while, it became constant, with my weekly paycheck going to Mama. I was also still in school, but that meant nothing to my mother regarding me. I would always get home late, requiring me to stay up even later to complete my homework, and finally getting into bed around 1:00 or 2:00 in the morning.

It was almost a year later, and on a Friday payday, that I made the conscious decision to run away once I received my paycheck. Mama was looking for me at the work place, but I had left early to live with some of the girls whom at that time I considered my friends. Some were from school, and others were from the streets. They all ended up being a bad group of teenagers. I went over to the home of a short, strong-headed girl named Erica Finch, who lived with her parents, Sandy and Robert, allowing me to stay with them for a while. However, Erica was a 14-year-old who didn't obey her parents. She usually slept in the same room where I was, but on this particular night, four weeks later, she wasn't there when I woke up in the middle of the night. I heard a strange noise and didn't understand what was going on. I thought it was her parents making the noise, so I didn't think anything else about it.

A week later, we were supposed to go hang out with teenagers our age. Erica let me know while we chatted in the bedroom that she couldn't make it, because something had come up. So, Erica left once she put her clothes on. Sandy was also not at home, and I didn't know at the time that Robert was at the store. Sometime later, however, Mr. Robert had come home. I guess he had sat around a little while, and then he went into the kitchen to cook breakfast. "Are you hungry,

Denise?" "Sure." I was a little nervous as to why we were here alone. "Where is everybody?" He told me, and then gave me a plate of food as he sat at the table with me. We began talking and eating at the table. A few minutes later, all I could remember is feeling weird in my head. Robert had given me a sedative in my orange juice, and I had passed out. When I woke up, I was in the bed without any clothes on, and Robert was gone. I wasn't sure what had taken place, because I didn't have a sex smell on me. But in my heart, I knew something wrong had happened to me again.

Finally, Sandy came home, noting that I was naked and in bed. "Is everything okay?" "Yes, ma'am." I said this because I couldn't remember anything. "I'm putting you in school tomorrow. Let's prepare for it." "Yes, ma'am, that sounds good." Everyone else came home later, and I told Erica about my feeling weird, passing out, and not remembering that I had taken my clothes off. "Are you all right Denise? Did you tell Mom what happened?" "No," I told her. We then started talking about other things, and went on about our day.

Two weeks had now passed since I was enrolled again in school. I woke up early one morning, and I heard the same noise. But this time was different, as I heard Erica's voice, and it sounded like she was in the room. I got out of bed, and went to the garage where Robert kept a bed. I opened the door a little, and my heart dropped into my stomach. Robert was having sex with Erica, and she wasn't fighting him off. All I could think of is that he had threatened her, and that he must have told her he would hurt her if she said anything. I quietly closed the door, and went back to our room, not knowing what to do next.

Erica finally came back to the room, arranging her clothes, and not giving away what I had seen. "Erica, where've you been?" "Talking to my dad," she said. "Are you sure?" "Yes, why do you doubt what I said?" I knew I couldn't ask her anything else. We took our baths, got dressed, and left the house for the day.

It was three weeks later, and I had just come back from visiting another mutual friend on this afternoon. I walked into the house, and, shockingly, found Sandy watching Robert have sex with their 14-year-old daughter Erica in their bed. My heart dropped into my stomach again, because she just sat there watching. She didn't even try to stop him from making Erica give him oral sex, or anything else he demanded. I hurriedly ran to our room, and I began to cry, trying to decide what to do. But someone had heard me in the house, and Sandy entered the room, pretending nothing was wrong. "Hi, Denise. How are you?" "Do you know where Erica is?" I asked innocently. "Oh, she'll be back in a moment." Finally, Erica silently and slowly

entered the room. I said, "Let's go for a walk."
"Okay, but I need to take a bath first, all right?"
"Sure." After her bath, she got dressed, and we
went to the park. Erica began to share with me
how tired she was of being forced to have sex with
her father. It had taken her several months after I
moved in to tell me. Although I had already seen
the answer to my question, I asked, "Does your
Mom know?" What came out next made my jaw
drop. "Yes, she watches us, and then she has sex
with him afterwards. I hate all of this." She then
proceeded to tell me, even more shockingly, that
her mother had initially set her up to be raped by
her stepfather by putting sedatives in her orange
juice. Once she was sedated, he raped her while
her mother watched. Erica had become
increasingly afraid of him over the years, and was
concerned that she had so many drugs in her
system from Robert's repeated sedative dosages
that they were affecting her brain. I told Erica that
we needed to leave the house. I never thought

about calling the police, because we had both witnessed the perpetrator threatening to hurt us if we told someone about the misconduct. We left with the intention to never return.

Staying in school, we went to the home of another friend from school, Shelia Brown, who lived with her attractive mother, Sharon, and her stepfather, Brian Brown, who had adopted her. Mr. Brown was tall, with a dark complexion, who seemed to be kind and friendly. We asked Shelia, a bright-skinned and intelligent young lady, if she could speak to her parents about our living there until we could find our own parents. It was about 4:00 p.m. when we finished our classes for the day. Mr. Brown and Sharon met us at the door of their house, and asked us to sit in the living room. Sharon locked eyes with us and peppered us with questions, curious as to where our parents were, and whether they knew that we had a friend who would allow them to stay with her in her family's home. We both told her that we didn't have any parents, and that we were concerned about our personal well-being. After a quiet moment, and then without any hesitation, Shelia's stepfather emotionally declared that we needed to have a roof over our heads. "I don't understand why any parent wouldn't attend to their kids. We can't leave them on the streets, Sharon. We have to let them stay here, and I will help you take care of them." Mr. Brown appeared extremely happy to give us a home, not questioning us about school, our grades, our medical issues, or any other important information that would concern us. However, Sharon was not appeased, continuing her line of questioning. "Do you girls have any bad habits? What do you girls eat? Are you and Erica sexually active?" Before either of us could answer, Mr. Brown interrupted. "Let's go to dinner. The girls must be hungry."

Shelia, Erica, and I were ecstatic that we were going to be living together. Erica and I were truly grateful to have a place to call our home. Also, for the first time in a long time, Erica and I felt safe. Shelia's family was very wealthy, so they took us to the finest restaurant possible. Mr. Brown had a six-figure salary working as an engineer, and for 10 years, Sharon had been the head of housekeeping at a fancy hotel. Although Sharon had a great job, she would often sacrifice her time, projects, and energy to accommodate Mr. Brown. Having the bigger income obviously made Mr. Brown consider himself the head of the household, and he wouldn't have it any other way.

Chapter Three

He left her with the understanding that he was a man to fear, with money and power. If she so much as opened her mouth, she was dead.

When dinner was over, Mr. Brown told Sharon to go home and that he would take care of all three of the girls. "Brian, I don't mind taking the girls home, because I have a meeting to attend at work, anyway." "Go to your meeting, and keep me posted." So, Sharon said goodbye to all of us, and told us that she'd see us later. Mr. Brown decided that he would surprise us girls by taking us shopping at the mall for school. After stopping at the ice cream counter in the mall, he told Shelia to "make those whores go to a store that sells sexy lingerie. You know what I like. Now get down there and make me happy." Shelia looked sad, but told him, "Yes, sir." He gave her $500 cash to pay for some items for us. Shelia smiled a little when she caught up with us. "Let me show you where I buy pretty underwear, since you two will need some." We laughed, and agreed, since we barely had anything to wear. I asked Shelia, "Do you get to go shopping a lot?" She said that she did. I told her she had a great stepfather, but she only said that he was okay. Erica didn't care much about anything except getting what she wanted, so we began shopping at the lingerie store. We looked at the negligees, buying several styles and colors. Afterward, Mr. Brown met us and bought us all some clothing and shoes to wear to school. Later, he made all of us an appointment at a beauty shop, and when were through, we all headed home with Mr. Brown. His wife worked overnight, so she wasn't at home.

Since the Browns lived in a very sophisticated neighborhood, their home had five bedrooms, allowing each of us to sleep in a separate room. We sat around, talked for a while, and then bathed. Right before we headed to bed,

Sharon called to talk to us. She asked if everything was okay. We talked about what we did at the mall, and told her about some of the things that we had bought. Thinking that we should not tell Sharon about our purchase, of lingerie, we finally hung up the phone, and everyone was off to bed. Since the house was very large, and the bedrooms were not adjacent to each other, sound didn't carry as well from one room to another, as in smaller houses. Of course, we appreciated Mr. Brown for being nice to all of us, still believing that he had our best interests at heart.

Three nights after moving into the Browns' home, I arose about 2:00 a.m. to use the bathroom. Walking past Shelia's bedroom door, all I could hear were the sounds of moaning and groaning coming from the other side. Thinking that Shelia might have had her television on, I returned to bed. The next morning, we got ready for school, and had a great breakfast that Sharon made for us.

That night, around 1:45 a.m., my bedroom door opened, and Mr. Brown appeared in the doorway. With everyone else asleep, he slowly entered the room, sat on my bed, and asked me how school was going. After I said it was fine, he chatted with me a little more, telling me how beautiful I was, and how I could come to him any time if I needed something. Abruptly shifting his tone of voice, he warned me not to speak of our conversation with anyone, because he was going to give me some money, buy me clothes, and anything else I needed. I promised not to tell anyone about the money.

Suddenly, he pulled the bed covers off me, and threatened me that something bad would happen to me if I said anything about our agreement, meaning that I would be out on the streets to live again. Turning the lights off, Mr. Brown forcefully put tape over my mouth and pulled off my panties. After putting on a rubber, he began having sex with me, causing me to cry, holding my arms down so that I couldn't move. When he finished, he left to take a bath. I continued to weep large, heaving sobs, and never told anyone what had happened to me.

When the next morning came, I didn't want to eat breakfast. However, I sensed that if I made a wrong move, this would cause problems, so I reluctantly forced down my food, and then left for school with Shelia and Erica, as usual. Two nights later, after our daily routine, Erica informed Shelia and me that Mr. Brown was taking her to the store. Mr. Brown strode into the room and told Shelia and me to finish our homework. After they left the house, Erica noticed with curiosity that they had passed the store without stopping. Instead, Mr. Brown drove her into a wooded area, causing Erica to inquire where he was going. "I have to make a stop before going to the store. Get out of the car." She obeyed, and they stopped by a cluster of trees.

He then began pulling Erica's clothes off, warning her that if she said anything about that evening that something bad would happen to her. "I'm the only one who can stop that. Do you understand?" Erica nodded fearfully, and said that she understood. He was aggressive with all women, and not just me. After removing all of Erica's clothing, Mr. Brown then he removed his own, compelling Erica to perform oral sex on him. But that was not enough, so he then forced her to lie on the ground and have sex with him.

He totally enjoyed raping young women. Since he had convinced his wife to get a night job, he wasn't having sex with her, making sure that she stayed out of his way. Because of her working nights, she didn't realize what he was doing during her working hours. Sharon had no real say in their home, and the job kept her busy with mandatory meetings. For years, Mr. Brown had been having sex with Shelia without Sharon being aware of it.

When Mr. Brown was finished with Erica, they returned to his home, after which he told her to clean herself up and go to bed, which she obeyed, while crying and trying to understand when this would stop. He left her with the understanding that he was a man to fear, with money and power. If she so much as opened her mouth, she was dead. Erica had been down that road before, and decided not to tell anyone, including Shelia and me. We had never shared details of our abuse by others, and none of us was sure what the others would think of us.

When Erica woke up the next morning, Sharon inquired if she were all right, noticing that she looked extremely tired. I eventually became interested in investigating who Mr. Brown really was, but I was also nervous about causing trouble. So, I stopped thinking about uncovering his background and continued living with the Browns.

Chapter Four

"You will do as I say, when I say it, and how I want it. Do you understand me?"

Two weeks after Erica's ordeal, I awoke at 1:00 a.m. hearing noises coming from Shelia's bedroom once again. I realized that Shelia was crying, and I wanted so badly to knock on the door, but I couldn't make myself do it. I figured that if Shelia wanted to share some information, she would. I therefore decided not to bother her. Shelia came down the next morning for breakfast, and didn't appear to be upset about anything. Sharon sat at the table with all three of us, asking about our day, and how we were being treated. We all stated that we were fine, and that we were really having a great time living together. But we were uncomfortable, because we all knew it was a lie. Sharon gave all three of us a hug, apologized for having to go to work so often, and for frequently attending so many mandatory meetings that took her away from home. We told her that we understood, and that we hoped she would get some time off soon.

Eventually, Mr. Brown entered the room, and asked, "How is everyone?" We all said that we were fine. As he ate his breakfast, he decided that he would take us to the movies, and then to dinner that evening. But before we got to the movie theater, Mr. Brown took us to a boutique, at which I noticed that he wanted me to get a special dress. In his eyes I was very pretty, and fine. He allowed Shelia and Erica to each select a dress. and then he chose one for me. At this point in time, I was only 14 years old. The dress Mr. Brown bought for me cost $450, and my shoes were $200. Next, he allowed us to buy whatever we liked that was presentable for school. We were then taken to a cologne store where Mr. Brown selected my fragrance for dinner and for the movie that night. Finally, as we were heading back to the house, Mr.

Brown asked Shelia and Erica to get out of the car once we arrived. He started rubbing up and down my legs after they left, and then, in a low and demanding voice, growled, "You are to keep your mouth closed about anything I say or do if you want to stay safe. And, by the way, you're my girlfriend. You will do as I say, when I say it, and how I want it. Do you understand me?" "Yes." "Go inside and get beautiful for me. I'll be waiting for you. Don't tell anyone, or it won't be good for you at all," adding, "I have people watching your every move, little girl." Feeling sad and fearful, I took the dress and shoes into the house. I couldn't talk to my friends about Mr. Brown's demands of me. So, we all prepared and dressed for the night's activities.

Once we had completed getting dressed, Mr. Brown came into my room, looking at me admiringly. "You look beautiful," he gushed, as he put his arms around me and kissed me. "I have somewhere to take you after dinner and the movie tonight." I gave him with an extremely concerned look, as he said, "I'll be waiting for you at the bottom of the stairs when you are done dressing." Mr. Brown brought the car around to the front of the house, and he, Shelia, Erica and I drove to an expensive restaurant.

When we arrived, our waiter mentioned to Mr. Brown that we all seemed nervous, to which he shrugged. We began ordering dinner, and I was trying to decide what to have from the menu. Before I'd made up my mind, Mr. Brown said to me, "You can't order anything fattening, because your body needs to stay looking good." He ordered a chicken salad with extra chicken for me, while my girlfriends ordered hamburgers with fries. Both girls looked at me, and asked me why I didn't order a hamburger with fries like they did. I simply stated that I wanted to try the chicken salad, and would probably order some fries later. I didn't want the girls to get suspicious, and I also didn't want to get in trouble with Mr. Brown. Shelia just thought it was weird for me to order a salad, because she knew that I loved pizza and hamburgers. To take the focus off me, I replied that I just wanted to try something different.

After everyone finished their dinner, we were finally heading to the movies. As we went in, Mr. Brown told me to sit by him. He encouraged the other two girls to sit in a row of seats in front of us. He told them that he wanted to watch me closely due to my medical issues. They looked at him strangely, because they had no knowledge of me having any medical issues. However, Shelia knew what her stepfather was planning for me. So, she said nothing, while she was sitting in front of us with Erica. Their silence was part of what we'd all learned from our past experiences. We didn't know whom to trust.

I sat with Mr. Brown behind the girls, and he began to rub his hands over my thighs and up my dress. I was shaking, which he noticed, and whispered to me, "Calm down. If you do what I say, nothing bad will happen to you. Do you understand?" I nodded. Continuing to slide his hands higher, Mr. Brown began touching my private area and started masturbating in the theater, while rubbing my private area at the same time. He had put his suit jacket over my lap, so no one else would see. Eventually, he whispered, "I got you something, and you'll get it tonight. I have to run to the car to change clothes, so tell the girls I'll be right back." I nodded at him, and then said okay. By the time Mr. Brown returned inside the theater, the movie was over, and it was time to go. As we were leaving the theater, Shelia and Erica asked me if I enjoyed the movie. I didn't say much, as I hadn't been able to watch most of it. I finally said, "it was okay." They both asked me, "What do you mean?" "Nothing," I said. We all got into Mr. Brown's car and headed home. When we arrived, Mr. Brown asked if we had enjoyed the night. We responded by saying, "Yes, thank you sir." Shelia, Erica, and I talked for a few minutes, and then Mr. Brown told them to go to their rooms and get prepared for bed. They told us good night, and left. I realized that all three of us were fearful of him. Entering my bedroom with me, he told me to take a bath and meet him downstairs. After we left the house, he drove me to a hotel in another city. I wanted to ask him a lot of questions about what was going on, but before I got out of the car, I noticed what I thought looked like a handgun in his pocket. Now I was even more nervous about the situation, but I kept my mouth closed.

We went to the front desk and checked in. As we went to our hotel room, the front desk clerk said, "You and your daughter have a great time. Enjoy your stay here." "We will." After we got to the room, he told me to undress. I was doing this too slowly for him, and he eventually started taking my clothes off himself. He then began having sex with me, which also included oral sex. I just lay there crying. I knew that Mr. Brown would have sex with me as often as he liked. He didn't care, or notice, how I, at 14 years old, would feel. He told me to take a bath after we were done so that we could head back to the house before Sharon returned. Looking me in the eyes, he said, "Sit down. I need to talk to you." Continuing, he said, "I have some other girls I help, because they don't have anyone to help them, girls like you and your friend Erica. No place to live, no clothing, or no food." I realized he was trying to put a guilt trip on me to cover up for his behavior. "There are some older girls who work for me that you will meet, so you'll stay with me at all times. The other girls will go to work and come see me. Okay?" This made no sense to me at that time. Later, when we went home, I went to bed. As I woke up the next morning, Shelia told me that she'd been looking for me last night. As I noticed Mr. Brown looking over at me sternly, I said, "I went for a walk; that's all." I noticed that Shelia was also looking at me. Glaring suspiciously at both of us, she rose from the table and went to her room.

Sharon was just getting home from work, and was trying to understand what was going on with Shelia, since she wasn't at the breakfast table. She headed to Shelia's room, but Shelia didn't want to talk about the situation. Eventually, she politely asked her Mom to leave her alone. I walked outside, and Erica followed me. She asked me if everything was okay, and I said everything was fine. But she persisted, and asked me, "What does that mean?" "Nothing." "Things sure are weird here at Shelia's, house, with her Mom never home at night." "Shelia says it's nothing new, because her Mom always worked really hard."

"That's right. Why don't we go back into the house? It's getting cold outside."

Sharon was already in her room asleep when we walked back into the house. I went to my room, sat on the bed, and tried to figure out the situation. I was just 14 years old, but things were getting more difficult for me every day.

Chapter Five

"She's not going to talk, she's my bottom whore,"
he informed him. I felt stupid, because I didn't
know what he meant by that.

Mr. Brown came to my room the next day, and again he made me have sex with him. He also mentioned again that he was taking me to meet the other, older girls that night. What I couldn't understand is that when he left for work, he was only gone for about 4 ½ hours if he wasn't going out of town. But I knew that he was an engineer. Didn't they work longer hours? Once I had heard Shelia and Sharon say that Mr. Brown made good money, so I was even more confused.

Around 9:00 p.m., Mr. Brown returned home and changed his clothes. He came upstairs and told me to come with him. Apparently, he had already spoken to the girls I was going to meet. We left, drove to another house, and I soon learned that it also belonged to Mr. Brown, with about 10 teenage girls living there. One of these girls informed me that she had been with Mr. Brown since she was nine years old. Her mother was on drugs and she'd never known her father. The Browns helped her by taking her in. She told me that she was 16 years old, and was being home-schooled by a lady that Mr. Brown paid to teach all the girls. I never said a single word to her, because I didn't think much of the matter. But I did think to myself that I had to keep going to school. Mr. Brown then entered the room, and introduced me to all the girls by stating that they worked for him. Finally leaving the girl's house, we went to go eat lunch.

After lunch, he took me to another house that I hadn't been to before. We walked into the house, and I was startled to see five men hanging out in the front room. Mr. Brown told me to sit down, and one of the men asked him, "Man, why did you bring her here?" "She's not going to talk, she's my bottom whore," he informed him. I felt stupid, because I didn't know what he meant by that, but it sure didn't sound good. I wished I understood the meaning of "bottom whore." However, I was too afraid to ask a bunch of questions. Mr. Brown always had a group of women around him, including his wife. As I sat there watching, I witnessed some type of white powder on the table that the guys were tasting. At the time, I had no idea of what was going on, but I knew that something didn't feel right.

About 25 minutes later, I left what was apparently a drug users' house with Mr. Brown, who began to reiterate things he'd told me before, but this time with a raging voice. "Do not tell anyone about the things I've shared with you. This is my business." "Mr. Brown, I understand. You don't have to scream at me all the time," I retorted. He started to relax a bit, and then he said, "Start calling me Brian instead of Mr. Brown." "Okay,

Brian, I got it." "Good." We drove back to the family house where Shelia and Erica were waiting. They heard us coming and came down to meet us at the front door. Shelia then asked Brian, "Where have you guys been?" "Don't ask where we've been, that's not an option around my house. Nobody gets to ask me that. My own wife doesn't even ask me that," he said intensively at Shelia. I turned and looked back at Brian before heading to my room, still extremely upset about the activities I saw that day. A few hours had passed when I overheard Brian and Sharon intensely arguing. I couldn't figure out why, but it seemed to me that it was really bad. I later heard Sharon walking out the front door crying, getting into her car, and driving away. Later, I decided to sit outside on the porch. Brian later showed up, and asked me to come to his car. When I got into the car, he just sat there, staring at me. Finally, he opened his mouth and said, "I love you, Denise." I just looked at him, because I was trying to grasp something to say in response to his confession. My mother had never used that word with me, and I was trying to understand what that truly meant. Brian explained it with his next breath. "If someone helps you, buys you things, has sex with you, and gives you a place to stay, then that means they really love you."

The more I was around him, the more I believed him. Sometimes, he gave me gifts, one of which was a $500 tennis bracelet, and another was a leather jacket. He would also make me do things with him, like going to pick up money up from drug dealers. While riding in the car transporting drugs and drug money, Brian would give me marijuana, and I would smoke it. He began giving it to me more often, and started making me drink a little. Later, I learned that Brian had already turned Shelia on to his illicit activities. She was partaking in prostitution, drugs, and drug sales and distribution. Then, like a house of cards in a hurricane, everything started to fall apart.

After Brian took me home one night to have sex, he demanded that I go to some private rooms with him. By this time, I didn't care anymore about anything going on in my life. Because I had been without love for so long, I trusted him more than anything, even more than my own mother. I had run away from home because I was horribly mistreated. I felt that she was more concerned about Anthony and Lenise, since she never even cared enough to try to find me. On the other hand, Joyce would do anything for them. Shelia and Erica also started hanging out in clubs around this time, and I began joining them. We bought fake IDs to get in, buying drinks and wearing little clothing, to attract the attention of grown men.

One night, Shelia met a guy who was 14 years older, exchanged phone numbers, and met later that night. The following night, we decided to hit the club again. I was sitting, dancing, and drinking once we got into the club. Several guys offered to buy me drinks, dance with me and take me out to eat after the club closed. Even though I was having fun at the nightclubs, I was still afraid of Brian hurting me. Shelia would tell the guys that I would get in trouble if I took their phone numbers. However, the guys left me their numbers on the table anyway.

Three hours later, Brian found out where we were, and came in looking for me. I happened to be on the dance floor with another guy when he found me. Brian rushed toward me, grabbed me, and pulled me out of the club. Taking me to an apartment where he'd obviously been staying for a while, he began to beat me with his leather belt, hollering that I was not to go out without him. My eyes and arms were swollen and bruised when he finally stopped. I was extremely upset that any man would hit me. Brian later hugged me and apologized for his actions.

After he apologized, I got up in his face and asked him, "Why did you do that? Brian, why?" He replied, "I love you too much, and I don't know what to do. When I saw you with that guy on the dance floor, I became angry. Baby, listen to me. Remember when I named all those things that show that I love you?" I nodded. "This is another way to show you that I love you." "But what about your wife, Sharon?" "I am not going to be with her after a while," he told me. I asked him why. "Because I love you so much, and I will give you anything if you listen." Curious as to his intentions with Erica and Shelia, I inquired, "What about them?" Continuing to try to defend his actions, he said that they would be out of our lives real soon. I asked him what he meant. "It means that you and I will have a happy life. You won't have to worry about anything. You will just go to school and not tell anyone about what we're doing. Do you hear me?" "Yes." "I mean it. Don't even talk to your teachers about us. I'm considering keeping you forever if you don't mess things up." "What could I mess up, Brian?" "By talking too much, Denise. You have a good life. Leave it that way, okay?" "Okay." Brian seemed to calm down a bit. "Come on, and let me clean you up. I'll get something for your eyes."

In the morning, we went to the drugstore so that Brian could buy medicine for my face. I went into the store wearing sunglasses and a hat to cover up what he did to me the night before. Returning home, Brian gently applied the medicine to my face himself. That afternoon, he went out to transport what I believed were drugs. When he returned, he came into my bedroom to give me a hug. He also wanted to have sex with me, so he told me to undress. By this time, Brian knew he could manipulate me into doing whatever he said without me questioning him. When he was finished with me, he got up to leave, and warned me not to answer the door or go out for anything.

Later that night, I received a page from Shelia asking me if I were okay. As I returned her page by calling her, she greeted me with, "Hello girl, how are you?" "I don't know." "Are you okay?" I started replaying in my head what Brian had said to me and replied, "I'm fine. Just hurting a little bit, and I need to lay down." "What do you mean?" I didn't tell her. "Have you heard from Erica?" She had been in the club last night when Brian showed up, disappearing about two hours later, and Shelia was beginning to get concerned. "I'm not sure, but it seems like something's wrong." "I haven't seen or talked to Erica since last night." I thought she may have been drinking, but I wasn't real sure. When that reality dawned on me, I felt the strong need to find Erica.

"How are you going to find Erica if you can't leave the house?" This was a detail that I had carefully confided with her. "I don't know, but I'm afraid that something may have happened to her." That was a scary thought. "I'll think of something. Maybe I'll ask Brian if he had seen her." "Are you crazy?" Shelia blurted out, with fear in her voice. "Why do you say that?" She said in a trembling voice, "Because there's a lot that you obviously don't know." "What do you mean by that?" "Just understand that you can't let Brian know that Erica's missing, and know that I can't tell you no more than that over the phone." "Well, how am I supposed to know what to do to help?" Shelia ignored my question. "When are you coming back home with Sharon and me?" "I don't know. I promised not to leave the house until Brian returned." "Where did he go? We should be trying to find Erica now." "I'm just as worried about Erica as you are, but Brian would be beyond upset with me when he returns if I wasn't here." I could not handle the consequences of disobeying Brian. Shelia didn't understand what I was talking about. "Denise, is something wrong?" "I'm fine. Page me later with the phone number where you can be reached." Shelia didn't feel good about any of this, with Erica being gone and I being unable to help her look for Erica.

"Erica has been acting strange lately, Denise. And you—you're crazy, girl, for being with a married man who won't let you leave the house." I rolled my eyes. "Shelia, just leave me a phone number, okay?" Brian was my man, he loved me, and he wanted to be with me forever. All I had to do was just go to school, sleep with him, and do whatever he said. Shelia persisted and demanded, "What is wrong with you? Something's just not right." I insisted that I loved Brian, because he bought me anything that I wanted, he didn't love Sharon, and that he was going to leave Sharon to be with me.

It was puzzling to me that Shelia didn't understand I wasn't going to leave Brian, so I began to cry. "Denise, stop crying. Everything will be okay." "I have to go. Brian is probably on his way back to the house." He would get mad if he found me on the phone when he got back. Sure enough, just as I got off the phone with Shelia, Brian walked through the door. I was sitting on the couch with an ice pack on my eyes, pretending that I hadn't done anything. Brian strode over to where I was sitting. "Denise, what have you been doing while I was gone?" "Nothing, Brian. Nothing at all, just like you told me." He eyed me suspiciously.

"Have you been talking to Shelia?" "No, of course not," I lied confidently. "I haven't been speaking to anyone, because you told me not to. I did what I promised." Brian seemed to accept my lie. "Okay, get into bed. I'm a little tired, but I still need to make love to you." "Sure, Brian, but I'd like to ask you a question first." Brian didn't like this at all. "Denise, why can't you just do what I ask without questions? That takes away from how beautiful you are, and how many times I let you have some of me." I smiled at him. "You're crazy, Brian." "Don't you like what I do to you? Don't you like how I make you feel, little girl?" "I'm not a little girl." "If you're not a little girl, then what are you? Because I only deal with women that do as I say." "I can be a woman, Brian, and do whatever you say," I assured him.

I was willing to do anything for Brian. I couldn't explain it, but I felt a strange liking and attraction for him, which I believed to be love. "I'm going to teach you how to be a real woman. First, you gotta do what I tell you. Then, I will do whatever I want to me, and you better like it!" He whispered in my ear, "Understand? You heard me bitch; do what I say." Later that night, I was lying in bed when Brian fell asleep, and noticed that his pager was on the coffee table, beeping. I looked at it, because I wanted to find out who it was, but I was also worried that Brian would jump on me if I ever touched his pager. Brian finally woke up, picked up the pager, and went to the phone. A minute passed when I realized that it had been another girl who had beeped him. I knew this when he said, "Hey, what's going on, young lady? Where have you been? I told you to meet me tonight. I got something for you." Listening to the conversation, I felt strange trying to figure out what was going on. Brian obviously had other women who were free to call him, but I was unable to do anything about it. Finally, I couldn't help asking him, "Hey, who's paging you?" To make it seem like it wasn't a big deal, I simply said, "I was just wondering, that's all."

Brian accused me of asking too many questions about his business. "You know damn well I don't play around when it comes to you being in my personal business without my saying so. Do you remember, I buy your food, send you to school and give you what you want?" "Brian, I know that you give me everything. That's why I always thank you for being there for me, even when my Mama wasn't. You came along and showed me you loved me. I'm never going to leave you for anyone else." "That's right, you don't bite the hand that feeds you," he asserted. "I want you to say, Brian, whatever you want me to do I'll do it." I repeated exactly what he wanted me to say. He responded with, "That's my girl. And, that's what I needed to hear. Now I have to go and meet someone who works for me. You'll meet her soon, and I want you to be extremely nice to her. She keeps me out of trouble." That someone who Brian was referring to was his Councilwoman, Kelly Washington, of Capital City. "Brian, don't worry. I'll be nice to her." He seemed to be satisfied with my answer. "Okay, I'm leaving for a while. There's plenty of food in the refrigerator and in the pantry. Don't leave the house or open the door." "What should I do if the girls come by?" "They won't be coming by. Just relax and do what I tell you." Brian left and headed to his meeting with Councilwoman Kelly Washington.

Chapter Six

Whenever he was tired of Councilwoman Kelly, he pulled a gun on her to make her do whatever he wanted sexually.

"Hello, Brian," she said. "How are you?"
"Counselor, I didn't come here for the small talk." Kelly, a gorgeous lady with long, brown hair, let him know that she didn't come for it either; she was just there to seal the deal. But, she suggested that they have a glass of wine first. "You may notice that I'm not wearing any panties." Brian then repeated, "Seal the deal?" "Yes." Brian pulled her coat off, and provided her with the services she was expecting. "I thought you'd never ask," she said. Whenever he was tired of Councilwoman Kelly, he pulled a gun on her to make her do whatever he wanted sexually. He slapped her, and as she started heading for the bedroom, he said, "Go take a bath, Councilwoman. You stink." Brian told her that he needed her to

keep her ears open, and to make sure he wasn't caught up with her. "I don't want the FBI to bring me down. Do you understand?" "You know I'll do whatever you want." He already knew that. "I don't need no main whore; I'm good taking care of my business." "I understand." Brian got ready to leave. "Look, I got to get back to my girl at the house, and go take care of things."

Brian headed back to the apartment he'd leased, so that we could live together. "Denise, what's going on?" "Nothing, Brian--really." I'd slept for a while, and then I woke up, since I was hungry. "Did anything special happen while I was gone?" "No, but someone came by and knocked on the door. I didn't open the door, but looked through the peep hole to see who was there. It was a black guy who looked like he was sick." It sure seemed weird, because Brian had told me that nobody knew we were living in the apartment. "So, what happened next?" "Well, the guy looked around, and then he left." "What was he wearing?" He wore a white T-shirt and blue jeans." Something about the guy at the door had seemed so strange to me, but what did I know? I was still trying to learn how to be a woman for Brian. He said, "That's right, I got you." But he began acting even more strangely.

"Denise, get up and get dressed. I'm going to take you somewhere with me. I'll be back in a few minutes. Right now, I'm headed to the store to get some cigars." "I promise, I'll be dressed and ready to go when you get back." However, Brian hadn't gone out for cigars. He had begun to realize that something wasn't making sense, especially after I told him about the man who had knocked on our apartment door. So, instead, he met with a guy who worked for him as a lead drug dealer. I had never been aware of these activities, because I still believed that Brian had a regular job. I didn't realize the danger I was in, and what it might cost me to escape it.

As the months went by, my relationship with Brian continued. "Hey man, did you take care of getting Erica over to her house?" Brian asked. Marcus Williams said, "Yeah, man." Marcus was a street hood who worked for him. "Did you pay off Sandy?" "Absolutely." "Man, I got this." "What's up with her? That chick is a freak." "I had her, man. She don't give a shit about Erica, even though I've been screwing her since she was 11 years old." Marcus asked, "How in the hell did you manage to do that?" "Sandy's a whore, and all she cares about is money. And I wasn't the only dude hitting that booty. Her father was doing her a long while, even before I started having sex with her." Marcus said, "Damn, man. I want some of that booty too. Young, and you can make her do whatever a dude want her to do. Shit. I'm getting hard just thinking about that young ass!" "Man, look. Tonight, go over to the house and act like I sent you over to see Erica. Tell Sandy somebody from her past is looking for her, because she slept with their husband." Marcus agreed and Brian continued. "And then have her get dressed so you can take her out, because she's so beautiful. Just lie to her, man. Hell, you know how to do it, man." Marcus agreed. "Yeah, I guess I am the man with the player's plan. And besides, before I put her to rest, I want some of that booty." Brian told Marcus that he didn't care what he did to Erica. "Just give that tramp's Mama some money and a little dope to keep her ass out of my business. Erica needs to disappear." "I got you, man. No problem."

Later that day, around 4:30 p.m., Marcus went into action. He called Sandy's house, and she answered after a few rings. "Hey, is Erica home?" "Yeah, who's calling?" "I am a friend of Brian's, and something has come up. The word on the street is that some woman was looking for Erica, and planned to hurt her because she had slept with her husband." Sandy seemed surprised. "What? When did that happen?" "A few months ago." "I already told Erica over and over again that she was going to get her ass whipped one day for sleeping with all those married men. What are you going to do about it?" "Brian's gang can take care of it." "All right, then. Come get Erica out of the house." "Yeah, and I got something for you, too." Sandy knew what this something was. "Yeah?" "Have Erica dressed and ready by 7:30 p.m., so I can pick her up." "Okay, but be sure not to forget about me." "Trust me—I won't forget you!" "You got a deal." At this point, Erica had no clue that Marcus would come for her that night.

Around 7:20 p.m., Marcus rang the doorbell, and Sandy answered the door. "What's up?" She seemed anxious. "Hurry up, and give me what you brought me. I need to go take care of some business." Marcus hesitated. "Say, is Erica going to leave with me? You know Brian don't play about his money." "Cool it. It's all under control, and Erica would do just as you said." "Alright, game time. Tell her to come downstairs and make sure that bitch has no panties on." Sandy called up to her. "Erica, come down, baby. You're getting ready to go out, and have some fun like I told you that you would." "Okay, Mom, here I come."

Erica came down the stairs looking like a high-class hooker, and saw Marcus. "Hello." Marcus was in a hurry. "Hello, whore. Let's go!" Erica turned to her Mom. "He's mean." "Girl, he ain't mean, he's just in a hurry to take you out and show you a great time." After giving Sandy $200 in exchange for permission to rape her daughter, Marcus took Erica to his car. She looked back at her Mom on the porch. "Bye, see you later."

After driving away, Marcus asked Erica what she liked to do for fun, and how old she was.

"I'm 15." He replied, "Yeah, just the way I like them." "Do you know Denise?" He growled, "I know that little whore—is that your girlfriend, or something?" "Yeah, Denise is my friend. Where is she?" "I don't know. I guess she's like you, getting laid, and soon to become MIA." "What's MIA?" Marcus laughed. "I'll let you know when that's being prepared." He had no concerns, remorse, or convictions of all the wrong things he had already done, as well as the wrong he was about to do. Marcus was driving Erica down Highway 45, heading south toward a town called Buffalo. He pulled off the road as the sun went down. "I have a surprise for you, Erica." Erica was pleased. "You do?" "Yes. Get out, and get it." She did as she was told. "Let's go over and get in those bushes. I know you like me, because I want to be your man." They began to walk toward a wooded area. Erica asked him how long they were going to be in the dark trees. "Until I tell you to stop." A minute later he told her to stop, and to pull her clothes off. "Right here?" Marcus said, "Hell yeah, right here." He pulled out a gun. "Do it now."

Marcus made Erica unzip his pants and give him oral sex. Next, he made her lie on her stomach while he rammed his penis in her booty. She began to bleed. Marcus then turned her over and had sex with in her. Finally, he injected some heroin into her arm, had her get dressed, and drove her back to Dallas. But he didn't take her home. Instead, he dropped her off in South Dallas on the corner of Birmingham and Oakland. Erica asked him, "Where am I?" "You're where you're going to make me some money, bitch!"

Chapter Seven

This girl, who was like a sister to me, ended up contracting HIV. It eventually turned into full-blown AIDs, and she died alone in an alley.

Erica had now become addicted to heroin, getting so high that all she could do was agree and ask if she could she have more of the "good stuff." Marcus gave her a little more heroin, and Erica began flagging down cars. Later that night, an SUV with five men stopped for her. Erica said, "Hey, can I go with you?" The driver said, "Hell yeah, you want all of us?" Erica said, "Sure." The men drove off with her, and took her to a hotel in Houston several hundred miles away. On the way there, every man who wasn't driving was having sex with her. When they arrived at the hotel, the men put her in the bath tub, cleaned her up, and laid her on the bed. Then they all started having sex with her all over again.

After they were finished with her, they dropped her off in the Third Ward. This was one of the city's most dangerous areas. She found an empty house for shelter, but she was raped again by some homeless men. Erica never returned home. This girl, who was like a sister to me, ended up contracting HIV. It eventually turned into full-blown AIDs, and she died alone in an alley. Her body was deteriorating in that alley for two weeks. Only then, due to the horrific odor, was she discovered. Nobody outside her mother was ever questioned or arrested regarding her death.

When Sandy was questioned, she insisted that Erica had been a disobedient child, and would never listen to anyone who tried to tell her right. She began to cry during the questioning to make people believe that she had been the perfect mother who had always protected her daughter and taken care of her. However, Sandy was selfish and greedy.

One night, Robert told Sandy to dress Erica up and bring her to their bedroom so that he could open her up, and that she would be his woman, too. Otherwise, he would leave and find himself another woman who could sexually satisfy him. "So, either you give me your daughter to screw, or I'm out, tramp."

Sandy had allowed Robert to rape Erica every night from the time Erica was 11 years old, because he was demanding and on drugs. Still, she loved him and would do whatever he said, even after he physically abused her.

Sandy agreed to his demands, begging him not to leave her. She would do whatever he wanted him to. Robert said, "Yeah. That's what I'm talking about. If you want to keep getting my penis, broad!" Sandy said, "I can't live if you leave me. I'll bring her to your room tonight."

"I'll be ready. And go get me some lubricated rubbers because I want to be easy on that fresh ass. Hurry up."

Later, Sandy brought Erica into her bedroom. Robert quickly undressed Erica and began with oral sex, then began to hurt her by raping her brutally. Sandy just sat there and watched all of this. He began raping her daily, and eventually she thought it was normal to sleep with her father.

When she became a teenager, she started sleeping with any man that demonstrated the same attitude as her father did. Later, all the men she didn't volunteer to sleep with showed her no respect.

Shelia and I were contacted and told that Erica had been found dead, after we had spent weeks looking for her. I began to cry when I heard the news, and asked Shelia, "What happened to Erica?" Brian heard me and said, "Ooh, I didn't know that. Denise, just leave it alone. That's why I didn't want you to hang around with those two girls, Erica and Shelia." I told him I would stop, and reminded him that I had done everything he'd asked me to do.

"Brian, I need some things. Will you take me shopping?" "Sure, but I need to make a stop first." "Thanks, I'll get dressed and get ready to go." "You put some shades on and represent both of us well, you hear me?" "I understand." I thought he was on his way out, but then he added "...and keep your mouth closed about other people's business." "No problem. I wasn't going to talk about anything to anyone." But I had no idea where my life was headed.

Chapter Eight

"I guess you don't really get it, Denise.

The only way you get away from Brian is

death."

"Come on, Denise, we have to go. I have a stop to make before taking you to the mall, and that will take a few minutes." "Okay, I'm ready." We left and headed out. Eventually, we arrived at a plain brick building. "Where are we, Brian?" "We're in south Dallas. Stay in the car, and leave the doors locked. I won't be too long." "Okay, Brian. I'll see you when you get back." "Yeah, just stay put right here."

Brian walked to the door of a building known as the South Dallas Projects and knocked on the door of a unit. He was carrying a briefcase, and I noticed that when the door opened, he was checked to see if he was "strapped," which meant carrying a gun. After the resident verified that Brian didn't have a gun, he let him in.

Brian was in the apartment for an hour, and I began to get nervous. I was trying to decide if I should get out of the car and see what was happening. Finally, Brian came out with his briefcase and another bag that looked like a duffel bag.

I had no idea what was going on, because Brian had always made me believe he was an engineer with a great job. He got in the car, placed the duffel bag on the floor and drove away, laughing and holding his stomach. I asked him what was wrong.

"Nothing's wrong. Stop worrying about me. I'm going to drop you off at the mall and Marcus will pick you up, baby." I asked Brian why he couldn't pick me up himself. "Because I have something to do. Denise, what's up with the 20 questions?" "It's just that I thought you said you planned to go shopping with me." "Here's $800. Go and buy something sexy because I'm taking you out tonight." He gave me a kiss and left me at a shopping mall in Oak Cliff. After a few minutes at the mall, I ran into Shelia.

"What are you doing, Shelia?" "I'm looking for something to wear at the club tonight. Are you coming, too?" "No, Brian said he was taking me out, but you know how that goes." "Yes, I do. Are you okay?" "Yes, but sometimes I wonder about Brian. It's probably nothing, but he's just acting a little strangely, that's all."

Shelia shrugged. "Well, that's Brian. Are you guys seriously dating?" "No, he's just helping me like he helped Erica and other girls." She disagreed. "No, he tolerates me and his wife, and he used to tolerate Erica, but she's gone now. Things seem so weird without her being around." "Yeah, everything appears to be different. I never really knew her whole story." "What do you mean?" "I never knew if she went through bad things at home that would have allowed her to act the way she did." Shelia sighed. "I guess you really didn't know."

Shelia shared with me the history of Erica's childhood and how she had been raped by her father since she was 11 years old, and that her mother had even dressed her up for him. "Hell, her mother had sex with Erica and the father on many occasions. Sandy would perform oral sex on her, and then on her father in the same day."

I was stunned. "What?" "Yeah, and her mother made her a prostitute for money and sold her to drug dealers for drugs." "Shelia, are you serious? I just thought things were different for you guys, considering I've been raped by family members and my mother's boyfriend, and all my mother cared about was me getting money from men to help her and my brother and sister who were living at home. My mother never looked at me as being a smart or decent young lady, because she always told me I would never amount to anything. I was trash to her, as she made me work and then would take all my checks until I finally got one of my checks and ran away the same day.

"My mother would buy whatever she wanted with my money, and I could never do anything for myself. She would tell me often that I was worthless until I brought her money, and if someone did something bad to me, she would say it was my fault, and would stop answering her telephone. I just wanted her love and for her to be proud of me, but instead she would continue to tear me down as a child, as she would tell other men about me at my auntie's club around the corner of our house in South Dallas on Clarence Street.

"My father at the time drove trucks and was always on the road, but sent money to help us. He was never married to my mother, because he was married to someone else he wasn't even living with; however, I've been mistreated since I was a small child. My mother wanted to get me out of the house, and told me that often. So, I ran away and she never called the police to make a runaway or missing person's report."

Shelia said, "That's just sad, Denise. I never knew you were treated that way, and I'm so sorry for you. How is school going?" I told her I was struggling and trying to decide if I were going to stay in school or not. Shelia said, "Brian tells me yes, you're going to stay in school." I nodded. "It seems like I have no one to trust but Brian."

Shelia looked at me warily. "Do you know him that well? Enough to trust him?" "Yes, I know him. We are good friends and he helps me with anything I need or want." Shelia said, "Denise, just be careful. Brian is a big-time drug dealer."

"What are you talking about, Shelia? He has a wife and other businesses, and he buys me anything I want because he has a great job. Don't talk about him, Shelia, he's dealing with a lot like me."

"Denise, are you in love with Brian? I promise not to tell anyone." "I can't talk about it, and you're lying about Brian. Stop it!" Shelia said, "Please, Denise. Listen to me. Brian raped me several times after so many other times that my own biological father raped me. Brian and I began to both think it was normal, and I started to like it. Brian would make his wife watch while he raped me in their own home, and she would go and buy me clothing and food to take care of me and send me to school. At this point, Brian had me around because I loved him and he knew it. Just like Erica. He raped her for years and she fell for him doing the same things, but when you're our age, maybe we can't make good enough decisions to live right.

"The thing about Erica was that she was so in love with him she started acting out a lot and Brian said he didn't like that. I think something would happen if someone would tell important people like our teachers or something. I don't know really, nothing at all may happen."

"Shelia, why did you say you loved Brian?" "Because ever since I was 12 years old, he had sex with me and I learned to like what he was doing to me, and he taught me a lot. But when he wants something else, you won't see him like you used to. Like me, he don't talk much to me now as I know he likes you, Denise." I said "No, it's not like that, Shelia. Brian is married and he loves his wife."

Shelia persisted. "You may believe some of that, but you don't want him with his wife, do you?" I insisted that Brian was married and he loved his wife. "I live in the house with Sharon.

She worries because she can't do anything against him or that she will disappear!"

"I'm not having this conversation, because it's not true, and he would be very unhappy," Sheila said. "If you love Brian, don't talk about him, just let things be. You hear me? Just let things be. Besides, although no one can prove all this stuff you're saying about the sexual encounters, you probably right. He always uses a condom on anyone other than his wife, but he takes care of them all, and makes his wife do that also." "I need to do some shopping now, because Marcus is picking me up soon, and I haven't bought anything yet." "Okay, but be careful, Denise. Brian is known everywhere because he is a member of the cartel, and it's the truth. Don't ever ask him about his business, because he will become extremely upset and may act out about it. Please, honestly, don't even tell him we talked."

"Okay, Shelia, I get that. But what I don't understand is that if that were the case, why are you still dealing with him?" "I guess you don't really get it, Denise. The only way you get away from Brian is death! And it won't ever be something he does himself." I didn't know whether to believe her or not. "I really have to go, Shelia." "I understand. Goodbye."

At this point, I had mixed emotions regarding what was going on in my life. I needed to deal with it without getting Brian upset, so I kept shopping as if I hadn't met Shelia, and bought some new dresses, pant suits and shoes. Two hours later, Marcus arrived to pick me up and take me to Brian. "Whoa, did you buy out the whole store, and do you have any money left?" I just looked at Marcus and smiled. "Where's Brian?" "He's in the hood, so stop worrying. I'm taking you straight to him. We should be there in 10 minutes."

I had no idea I was riding in a vehicle with $20,000 worth of guns and $50,000 worth of heroin, a drug known on the street as "smack." Not being totally tuned in with my surroundings, at 14 years old, I still had a lot to learn.

Chapter Nine

"Denise, this cost me a G. I don't want to hear about you losing it. Are we going to have some problems?"

Finally, we arrived in South Dallas. Brian was at a gambling shack. Marcus took me inside and Brian had his hat on backwards. It was apparent that he'd been drinking heavily.

Brian called out, "Come here, baby. Ain't my girl fine as hell? You clowns better not answer that, or I might have to get on all your asses. Don't look at my baby, I don't play that shit." He turned to Marcus. "Where are my girl's shopping bags at?" "Denise, what did you buy today?" "I got some dresses, pant suits, shoes and underwear."

Brian exclaimed, "That's my girl. What stores you go in? You know I don't let you wear cheap things." "I went to Dillard's, Lane Bryant and Neiman Marcus." He seemed pleased. "That's right, you're going to be on my arm, you can't be raggedy." He stopped and reached for a small box. "I bought you something, Denise." It was a necklace, and he asked me to put it on. "Denise, this cost me a G. I don't want to hear about you losing it. Are we going to have some problems?" I shook my head.

After sitting in the gambling shack with Brian for a while, a woman walked up and asked to speak to him. I was upset but said nothing, as I remembered what Shelia said about how Brian would respond. So, I just stood there until Brian ordered me to walk away, which I did. But I could still hear their conversation.

Brian inquired, "What's up, Kimberly?" "I brought you the money, Brian." "How much?" "Thirty thousand dollars." He didn't like her answer. "Where's the rest of my money, bitch?" "Brian, I'm doing the best I can. Really!" She looked frightened. "You don't understand…that ain't good enough. You have until this afternoon to come up with the rest of my money, or there's going to be trouble. You understand me?" "Brian, it's not right. You don't make all your girls get out and work and make you money."

"Are you talking about anyone in particular?" "I'm just saying you have most of your women doing everything, and you have two doing nothing but shopping." Brian responded, "Whore, stay out of my business. My wife works and my girl ain't going to do nothing but keep me happy. You need to set your old ass down somewhere and figure out how to get my other $10,000 on my dope. Now get the hell out of my face."

He turned to some men standing at the door. "Get this tramp out of here, security." He turned to me. "Come here, baby. You ready to go?" "Yes, Brian." "Let's go, then."

We got in the car, drove down Highway 75 North Central Expressway, and headed home to the condo. When we arrived, Brian received a call from Sharon. She said that she and their children were moving out of the house because he never came home to spend time with her since I had moved in. She was tired of it, and just wanted out after 36 years.

The truth of the matter is that she knew the FBI was getting close to Brian, and she wanted to be out of his life when everything happened, from Brian getting busted for drugs and guns and from being the kingpin over all of the organization. It would eventually be found out that he was raping young girls. She always knew about it, but had never said anything about it.

Brian responded to his wife's news. "What's going on with you, Sharon, and what are you talking about?" "Brian, I'm tired of coming last in your life, and hearing you complain when I ask you to do anything. I just want my freedom to do whatever I want to do without you in my life. Since that girl's been around here, all you do is spend time with her, buy her expensive things like clothing, jewelry, and anything else she wants and don't want. Go on, marry her."

Brian retorted, "I don't know what all of sudden brought you to this place but what do I know? You're trying to handle the wrong dude. You know I don't play those games, all this I'm leaving and implicating my girl in all this. She don't have nothing to do with this. You been down for years on me having another woman, but now you being brand new about the situation, really?"

"Brian, I know I've been down over 30 years because I wanted to live good and for you to be happy. But I can't take it no more. It's either me or her." "Let me tell you something broad, you don't ever give me an ultimatum. And keep Denise's name out of your mouth, understand?"

"Yeah, I understand." "Now, you do what I tell you to do. Clean up the house. I'll call you when I finish taking care of Denise."

Sharon agreed, obviously afraid of the power this man had on the street. She had witnessed many murders over the years, and had never reported them to anyone, since Brian was also a part of local organized crime. No one could run from him, as he was on everyone's payroll, including the judges. Sharon knew what she would be up against, so she stayed put. On the other hand, I didn't know what Sharon knew, but I was getting ready to learn real soon.

Chapter Ten

"Damn, girl, when you going to learn how to cook?"

Later, I heard Brian talking to Marcus. "Hey, Marcus, what's up?" "Nothing. What's going on with you, fool?" "I need you to keep an eye on the hiz house. Feel me?" Marcus said he would. "Anything strange happen, change the game." Marcus said, "Yo. Done."

Sharon may have known her husband was having her watched, because she knew Brian well. She understood that people who had crossed Brian didn't walk away just because they wanted to. They usually had to suffer.

"I have to check on Denise. I'll holla at you later, bro." "Alright!" Marcus left. It was getting late. "Brian, I'm hungry. Can we get something to eat?" "Damn, girl, when you going to learn how to cook?" "I can cook some stuff." "Like what?"

"I can cook corn bread, pork chops, meat loaf, beans and sandwiches." Brian was amused. "Okay, I'll give you a little more time before I try your cooking." "That's fine, I'm hungry."

Brian took me to eat at a restaurant in Oak Cliff. He noticed Sharon's car across the street, and she was sitting inside it, watching us. Brian told me to go in and have a seat, because he already had guys in the restaurant waiting for us to enter. However, another one of Brian's bodyguards informed the persons inside that I was coming in alone. I went in and ordered a cold drink while waiting for Brian to come inside.

Brian walked across the street and watched Sharon as she got out of the car and began talking to a man. Apparently, Sharon didn't know who the man was, because she was trying to put a hit out on Brian and had no idea that her house, phone and car had already been bugged by the FBI two days before she told Brian that she wanted out of the marriage.

The man Sharon had contacted to set up Brian was a friend of Marcus, Roberto. Marcus had contacted Brian and he gave him some instructions, so Marcus let Roberto pretend to go along with the plan. Sharon thought she was paying a real hit man to get rid of Brian.

Marcus went out to the car, put on some gloves and cut the brake lines on the front of Sharon's car. When she drove away, she would eventually drive down a hill. With no way to slow down or stop, would have no control and crash.

After their meeting, Roberto prepared to walk Sharon back to her car. "Thanks for meeting me." "No problem, ma'am." "So, are you sure this is going to work?" "Listen, I am really good at my job. Are you sure this is what you want done?" "Yes, please, I never want to see him again." "It's a done deal. Can I walk you back to your car to make sure you're safe?" Sharon paid Roberto $20,000 to murder Brian and get him out of everyone's life. Starting her car, she began coasting down the hill. She was unable to stop at the light, and as the car went out of control, she began screaming and crying for help. But it was too late. Sharon was gone.

The police contacted Brian about the accident, because the car was in Sharon's name, and her family members suspected foul play. "I haven't seen Sharon for several days. I gave her money for the kids, but we aren't living together anymore." The detectives gave Brian their business cards. "We'll be in touch if we have more questions." "No problem, detectives. You know how to find me."

The investigation continued for two months, without discovering any evidence against Brian. But the FBI had been watching him for 20 years, and the evidence they needed to catch Brian was proving almost impossible to obtain, because he never really got his hands dirty by purchasing heroin or guns himself. And even though they suspected Brian of raping underage girls, they were having trouble getting evidence. You see, Brian never hugged, kissed or embraced me or other girls in public. When he had sex with them, he used lubricated condoms for extra protection, being careful not to leave any sperm available for testing within these young girls.

But back to that evening.

Chapter Eleven

"You're going to a grownup jail where they will do

all kinds of mean things to you."

I was still waiting for Brian in the restaurant, and he finally entered. "Brian, are you ready to order?" "Yes, Denise, go ahead." After we ate, we headed to a private club and had drinks. We eventually left around 2:00 a.m., and drove to another location, an apartment Brian had in south Dallas, right off of Martin Luther King, Jr. Boulevard. Although we were only supposed to have stayed there a few minutes, it took Brian so long to do what he was doing--counting money--that I fell asleep. Later, so did Brian.

Someone knocked on the door 30 minutes later, and it was Brian's brother Kendrick and his girlfriend. I eventually learned that he had been keeping the drug house at this location for years.

Brian said, "Man, where the hell have you been?" Kendrick replied, "Go on and leave man, we good." "No, Denise fell asleep so I'm going to stay until about 6:00 a.m., then head to the house." "All right. I'm headed back." By this time, I was half-awake. Brian asked him where his lookout men were. "They coming up." Brian said, "Tell them to pay attention." "All right. 6:00 a.m."

Suddenly, Brian said, "Do you hear that?" He grabbed his gun but couldn't get to it soon enough. The police and FBI had kicked the door in, and ran through the apartment. I could hear people screaming and the police shouting, "Freeze! Police!" I was baffled, and really didn't know how to handle all the mayhem. Everyone had been handcuffed except me. The police knew something was not right about the situation. After arresting everyone else, they sensed that I was a minor who had run away from home. A policeman asked me my age. "I'm 19 years old." "What is your date of birth?" I gave them the date I'd been using over the years. A female officer asked me again how old I was, but by then I had decided not to say anything else.

Brian was being led out in handcuffs, and I noticed he was looking intently at me. The female officer continued her questioning. "What is your name?" I decided to give her a fictitious one. "Okay, you're going to a grownup jail where they will do all kinds of mean things to you."

I thought about it for a minute, and decided to give them my real name and date of birth. The police contacted my sister, Sherry, a sister I hadn't grown up with, who had reported me as a runaway a few months prior to all these events.

The police took me to the Lee Todd Center for runaways, where they kept me for a week until Sherry came and got me out. The director of the Center was concerned about where I would be staying, as well as the relationship I had with my mother. Sherry told the director that my mother and I had no real relationship, and if I were sent back to her, I would continue to run away because we didn't communicate with each other at all.

The director decided to allow Sherry to take me home with her, as they had tried to reach out to my mother, but she would never return their calls. Later, I caught the bus to the apartment I had been living in with Brian. The door was padlocked, and a sign on the door warned sternly that no one could enter because of a federal investigation. Brian had property in other people's names, but not mine or other minors, as he never wanted anyone to know that he was sleeping with 11- to 15-year old girls, making them do whatever he wanted.

Brian stayed in jail for eight months before his trial and conviction. He was given a life sentence for drug trafficking, intent to sell drugs, the murder of his wife and over 20 other young women, 27 counts of child molestation, money laundering, and interfering with a federal investigation. I remember crying when he was sentenced, because I felt like he was the only person who took care of me at this point in my life. He had left me because people had lied about Brian.

I asked Sherry, "Why did they take Brian away from me?" "Denise, he was doing a lot of bad things." "No, he wasn't. I hate the people who did this to him." "Denise, you're 14 years old. Brian was too old for you, and you were on the way to getting killed. Do you not understand that?" "Brian would never hurt me. Mama hurt me often, but Brian never did." Sherry sighed. "Look, Denise, you're going to stay with me for a while and everything will be okay." I told her that I didn't want to stay with anyone, and for sure I didn't want to see my mother. "Stop talking nice to me, Sherry. You know our mother doesn't like me. She just likes what I can give her, that's all. I want to go see Brian." Sherry said, "I can't let you do that." "Why not?" "Because you're not old enough to be dating that man." I said, "Brian loves me, and he didn't let people hurt me. Nobody." I began to cry. "Please, I have to see him." "Denise, the FBI has talked to me about all this, and they told me the details of all the horrible things Brian has done to not only you, but also to 26 more young teenage girls, raping them at early ages, buying them things to stay quiet, and putting many of them to work as prostitutes, selling heroin and guns for him."

I tried to blink back my tears. "No, Brian loved me. Y'all made him leave me. My Mama don't care nothing about me, she just wanted me to get money and give it all to her." The FBI had coordinated with a state judge, recommending that I seek counseling. I was one of the 28 girls who had survived a relationship with a Mafia man.

Chapter Twelve

"He had his hand over my mouth so I bit him and started screaming, and his wife came into the living room where I was sleeping."

I went through a lot for a while, sorting through trust and anger issues, isolation from others, and a lack of educational learning, because Brian had been smoking marijuana and had supplied me with it daily. That was another way Brian kept control over my mind. When I was about to turn 15, I left Sherry's house, because there was a man there who wanted to sleep with me. Sherry knew it, and sometimes she would sit me down and say, "He wants to give you some money. Girl, I'm going to tell him you're going with him." "Sherry, I can't believe you're saying that. No, I'm not going with him!" "You gotta do something, because you don't have any money. I retorted, "I'm not leaving with that old, broken-down funky man." "Then what are you going to do, girl? Because you need a job." Sherry had made up her mind to stay in the house with Mrs. Manson, the lady who had raised her, and her husband, even though he was an alcoholic. One night, I was asleep in the living room when I woke up and realized that someone had crawled on top of me. I woke up and Mr. Manson had his hand over my mouth. I bit his hand and screamed, and Mrs. Manson came into the living room. She turned on the light and said, "What's going on?" I said, "He's trying to rape me." Sherry came into the room and told me, "Girl, stop lying. Mama told me you would do that." Mrs. Manson didn't agree with Sherry, saying, "She's not lying. Look! My husband has his clothes off, but Denise is still dressed."

Mrs. Manson put her husband out of the house, and told him he couldn't come back for a while. I didn't understand at the time why Sherry became angry and began shouting at me. "You have to get out! You had my daddy put out!" I didn't argue, and began looking for a place to live. Later, I found out that Sherry and her adopted father had been having sex all the time when Mrs. Manson wasn't at home.

Eventually, I ran into a cousin who worked at a fish place in South Dallas. Before this happened, I had been walking around Oak Cliff with nowhere to go. I had stopped by a club near the skating rink on Southern Oaks, and my cousin called out my name as I went in. He saw me because the person who owned the fish place also owned the club I had gone into. I stopped to see what he wanted.

"Hey, girl, where you been?" I recognized my cousin, Donnie. "I been around, cuz. What you been doing?" He said he was working. "I stay around the corner. How is your Mama?" "I don't know. She wanted me to move in with somebody, as long as it wasn't her house." Donnie looked surprised. "Wow, she doing that?" "Yes, cuz, it's all crazy."

Donnie asked me where I was staying, and I said, "Nowhere right now. I just left my sister Sherry's house, who was staying with the lady who raised her, Mrs. Manson. Last night I woke up and Mr. Manson was lying on top of me naked." Donnie said "Word! That dude was on some stuff. What the hell?"

"He had his hand over my mouth so I bit him and started screaming, and his wife came into the living room where I was sleeping. She told that fool he had to get out of the house, then my sister started tripping, talking about how I was lying. Then Mrs. Manson said I wasn't lying, as I had my clothes on." Donnie said, "Damn, cuz. That's messed up. You can stay with me until you get on your feet."

"Are you sure? I need a job, and I'm still looking for one." "Cuz, all you need to do is help me with the light bill and go to school." The house was paid for, as it belonged to his old lady. Donnie said, "I'm cool with that family, and when you're ready, let your mother know where you are." "That's cool, but right now I don't want to talk to her or any of them. You take me to the house, cuz." "Yeah, you ready? Because I have to get back to work in a little while." "I'm ready."

As we headed to the house, I wasn't sure how I felt about the situation right then, because there hadn't been a lot of positive things happening in my life. It had been filled with hurt, pain and people who were untrustworthy. All of this had taken a mental toll on me, and often I considered throwing in the towel. I didn't know that someone was praying for me.

Donnie said that the house wasn't much, but that I was welcome to it. I thanked him. "Where are your clothes?" "I didn't have much, since almost all of my clothes were still locked up in my old apartment that the FBI had locked down after they took my boyfriend to jail. The police said he had drugs and guns, and was raping me. That's crazy, for real." "Cuz, we don't have to talk about all that right now, as I heard a little bit about it already. But we'll make it through together, I promise."

I began to cry, grateful to my cousin, and thanked him for giving me a place to sleep in my time of need. Closing eyes, I finally got some much-needed rest, because I felt safe. When I woke up, Donnie went out and bought me breakfast, gave me $20 spending money and told me to have a great day. He also said he'd help me find work the next week if I needed help.

The next week, I found a job at a hamburger place and started working immediately, so that I could help my cousin with the bills, buy some clothes and save a few dollars for a rainy day. Donnie was encouraging me. "Cuz, keep going and you'll be fine." A month and a half later, he took me to the fish place with him to drop off some food from the other location, and his co-worker Wayne came out to the van to help Donnie load the food. Then his eyes noticed me.

"Donnie, who's that?" "That's my cousin, man, and she's been through a lot." "Can I meet her?" "Let me talk to her first." "Okay, thanks." "Man, I thought you had a lot of girls." "Yeah, man, but not the kind you want to marry." "Okay, so why do you have them?" "They all offer me something a little different from each other. But if I found the right one, I would let the rest go." "Bullshit! But if you believe that, who am I to say something different?" "Come on, man, she's young and cute. Give me a chance." Donnie said, "Man, you do all that, because I know you well."

Chapter Thirteen

Brian began to cry. "Baby, don't leave me here, please." Ten minutes later, he slumped down, turned his head to the right and stopped breathing.

A week later, I left to go to South Dallas where my sister Barbra was running a cafe on Oakland Boulevard. We were sitting and talking about the girls who worked for Brian and sometimes came into the cafe. I believe he paid them well for all their services. Then Councilwoman Kelly saw me and said, "I'm sorry for your loss," I responded. "What loss? I don't quite know what you're talking about." "I'm talking about Brian." "What about him?" "He's in the ICU." What's that?" "It stands for Intensive Care Unit, and that's where doctors put someone who is about to die."

I screamed, "No!" and began to cry. "Why didn't someone tell me this before now?" "Because Brian couldn't be around for you." "I don't care—I have to know where he is!" "He's at Parkland Hospital. Please be careful, because you shouldn't be there." "I know this, but I'm going anyway. No one is going to stop me!"

I called around until someone told me which bus to catch to Parkland, and I burst into his room just before they took Brian off life support. There were others in the room, and I thought I would be asked to leave, but someone must have recognized me. He asked everyone else to leave the room so I could say my goodbyes.

Everyone left, and I could see that Brian had tears in his eyes. "Brian, I love you so much! I'm staying with my cousin Donnie, and he's treating me just fine." Brian began to cry. "Baby, don't leave me here, please." Ten minutes later, he slumped down, turned his head to the right and stopped breathing. The doctors came into the room and told the family that they were sorry, that Brian had passed, and that the chaplain would be down shortly. It was not until sometime afterward that I learned that Brian, having been sentenced to 99 years in prison, was stabbed multiple times in the chest and neck because someone on the street passed the word to the prisoners that he had been sleeping with underage girls.

Later, I found out that Brian had two daughters, Janet and Patricia, living in another state, who had come to Texas to make the funeral arrangements. As I met them, they told me that Brian had told them about me. Janet said, "He loved you so much, because you were special. He didn't want to leave you with nothing, so he gave me something to give to you." I followed them to their car and they gave me a package. Crying continuously, I thanked them and clutched the package under my arm.

I didn't know why all of this had happened to me. I wasn't a bad person, and I didn't know what I was going to do now that Brian was gone from my life. His daughters shared with me that they understood how I felt, but that their father had not been in a position to offer us a life together because I wasn't old enough. According to state laws, he could have gotten into trouble for being with me, and they were sorry I wasn't aware of this.

Janet said, "No matter what, we want to thank you for making our father happy. We'll never forget you." We hugged and said our goodbyes, and they drove away. I walked to the bus stop and decided to open the package while I waited for the bus to arrive. The package had $10,000 of cash inside. $10,000!

Chapter Fourteen

"To do better, I want you to always remember that to do better is to gain."

The bus arrived, and I got on and went straight back to my cousin's house. Nobody was home, so I called him and asked him to come home for a few minutes because I really needed to speak to him. When Donnie got home, he asked me, What's wrong?" "Nothing, but I met Brian's daughters, who gave me $10,000 on behalf of their father. I want to give you $2,5000 to help pay for your support and for letting me stay with you until I find a job. I know that, although we don't have any bills right now, the money will help when you need it." Donnie hesitated. "Denise, this is a lot of money." I said, "Please, just take it and consider it rent for about three months." "Okay. You got it. Thanks, cuz, for real."

"No problem, Donnie. It's the right thing to do, since we've both been through a lot so far. I have a lot to learn quickly, without a mother or a real guardian to help me. Things will get better, because I think I finally have a true family member on my side." Donnie said, "I love you, cuz. You're going to make it and I'm going to help you." I said, "I went through more people hating and mistreatment, but it will be a brighter day one day."

Five months later, I was crossing the street in front of Donnie's house when I noticed a guy looking at me. I recognize him as someone who worked with Donnie, Wayne Henderson. He called out to me. "Hello, lady. How are you doing?" "Hello. I'm doing fine." "Good to see you again." "Good to see you, too." "Can I come and see you sometimes? Maybe take you out?" I didn't say yes or no. "Are you married, and do you have any kids?" "I've never been married and don't have any kids. Is that okay with you?" I smiled. "Yes." He said, "Just in case you've

forgotten, my name is Wayne, Wayne Henderson."
"I'm Denise Brown." "Okay. Can I visit you at
Donnie's house? I'm often there anyway." "Right
now, I need a little time, but we can talk for a little
bit. I'm trying to get my life together. If it weren't
for Donnie, I'd be homeless, with no job. Still, I'm
barely making it now." "Do you have any
children, and are you married?" "No, maybe one
day I'll get married, but I don't know. I need to
finish school first, and I'm really struggling with
my studies."

"Denise, I know I don't know you, but I've
known Donnie all my life. I have a lot going on in
my life, as far as getting myself together and doing
right in a relationship. But I'm 18 1/2 and I don't
have anyone serious in my life right now." "I hear
you, but I need some time to think about it."
"Okay, but you know I'm still going to try to speak
to you and take you out every time I see you."
"All right. I have to go. See you later." Wayne

looked disappointed. I had so much going through my mind that I couldn't get focused as quickly as I would have liked to.

A few weeks later, I started hanging out in clubs and drinking with a couple of other, older ladies and using a fake ID to get in. The older group of women was not great role models, living together in a house, with basically anything going on there. Different people spent the night and did anything else that wasn't right, including smoking and shooting rugs.

One night, I spent the night at their home, and was awakened at 4:30 a.m. by loud screaming and crying. The woman who owned the house was in the back room with a young girl, whom I believed to have been about 17 years old. She had come in while I was asleep and was taken to the back of the house in a room with six guys and the woman of the house, Mae.

I looked in and Mae and the six men were raping the young lady, while she was crying. Mae put her hand over the girl's mouth and I heard her say, "I asked you to just give it to me and you refused, bitch." I immediately got my things and left the house, then told a neighbor, who called the police. They showed up and knocked on the door and another visitor answered. The police asked, "Who is the owner of the house?" The man who had opened the door told them to hold on but the police came in. They stormed through the house and found the girl, and since everyone was naked, the adults were arrested for rape of a minor. They all were extremely upset, and they weren't sure who had turned them in, because no one ever saw me standing back there.

I thanked the neighbor, Mrs. Ella, for calling the police. "I have been raped most of my childhood by grown men, who they told me they would hurt me if I told anyone. I was beaten often at 11-15 years old without a parent to protect me. I really thank you." Mrs. Ella said, "Honey, I've seen a lot in my days, and some of the young ladies didn't live to give their testimony." I asked her what a testimony was. "Baby, when something happens in your life, whether it's negative or good, the result you're looking for is improvement. To do better, I want you to always remember that to do better is to gain."

I told her that I would remember what she told me. "Young lady, get yourself together. There's nothing on these streets but trouble, remember that. Someone will always be coming to harm you. Just stay out of the way of people you get a funny feeling about. Don't hang around all that. Dismiss your presence. Listen, someone has it out for you, so be careful." I told her that I didn't totally understand what she was talking about, and that I wasn't going to let people hurt me anymore, and I meant it.

Mrs. Ella said, "No, listen. Stop speaking those words because they will come into your life, daughter. Just be patient." "I will. Thank you, Mrs. Ella." "No problem, honey."

I never realized that Mrs. Ella practiced witchcraft and that she could see something in my future that was going to be pretty tough on me, but I would endure. The spirit of Baal would pass.

Walking away, I wondered what could possibly happen, so I decided I was just going to head home. I took a bath and thought about what Mrs. Ella had mentioned to me, becoming a little confused because things weren't quite making sense to me. I was sure that after thinking about all my past experiences, it surely couldn't get any worse.

Chapter Fifteen

"Why do you want me?" "Because I want a wife and some children." I asked him, "How do you know I'm the one, Wayne?"

A few days later, Wayne showed up at Donnie's house. "Denise, is Donnie home?" "Sorry, Wayne, but you just missed him. I'll ask him to call when he gets back home." "That's fine, but I also want to talk to you, Denise." "No, not right now." But he persevered. "Denise, please, I've been trying for months." "Okay, Wayne. What do you want?" "I want you to go out with me." I thought about it for a moment. "All right."

"Tonight, I'll take you anywhere you want to go. What do you like?" "Soul food would be good, but honestly, I don't feel like going out. But I'm willing to try a restaurant you may have in mind." "I'll see you at 7:30 p.m. I hope you can be ready by then."

He showed up on time to pick me up, and I was concerned that Wayne might have a crazy girlfriend or something similar going on. I just wasn't sure about Wayne. He was different after we left the house. When we arrived at the restaurant, we began to talk about our past relationships and what we could have done better. "Do you like this restaurant?" "It's nice." Abruptly changing his tone, he got serious. "I know you may not be ready, but I need a woman of my own. I've been meeting all these old, crazy women, but I want you."

"Wayne, I've heard that you've had a few women—actually, more than a few. Why do you want me?" "Because I want a wife and some children." "How do you know I'm the one, Wayne?" He didn't hesitate to answer. "Because you're different. I don't understand it, but you're different and beautiful and fine, and don't forget bright." I hadn't expected all this. He said, "Just let me be your man. I will help you."

After that night, we began dating for about six months. I could go everywhere with him, with no problems. Wayne finally asked me to go to his house with him and meet his mother, Minister Alice Henderson. We headed to his mother's house so he could introduce me to her.

Chapter Sixteen

Mrs. Alice asked me, "Baby, do you know the Lord?" I told her, "Well, I used to go to church, first with my Mom, and later with my brother and his wife."

When we arrived, Wayne's mother was sitting in a recliner singing about the Lord, and how He was a way maker and a heavy load carrier. She had the biggest smile ever.

Wayne walked in and said, "Hey old lady, this is my friend, Denise. She's Donnie's cousin." "Hello, Denise. Where are you from?" "It's a pleasure to meet you, ma'am. I'm from Dallas." Curious to know more about her son's girlfriend, Alice asked, "What about your family?" "My mother, Joyce Brown, is from Waxahachie, and my father, Michael Windstar, is from Bryan, a town in Texas. Since he drives trucks for a living, he was never really home with us, and he was also married to another woman, who had left him for another man. It's complicated."

I went on to tell Alice, "My mother never protected or supported me the same way she did my other siblings. All total, I have 11 brothers and sisters, and they each had their own ways about life. I'm still in school, but struggling with my studies, because the only honest person at this time in my life is my cousin, Donnie. He allows me to stay with him because my Mom wants me out for good."

Mrs. Alice asked me, "Baby, do you know the Lord?" I told her, "Well, I used to go to church, first with my mom, and later with my brother and his wife. So, I have heard of the name of Jesus but have never become close to Him."

Wayne came back into the room and appeared impatient. "Denise, are you ready to go?" I found out that Wayne grew up in church and had attended almost all of his life, but now he had no interest in church functions, or even going. However, he respected the idea of his mother attending, but secretly hoped she didn't ask him to go with her, so that he would never have to say "no" to her.

"Your mother is really nice." He shrugged. "She's okay." I laughed. "No, she's really cool." "I gotta go to work later. Do you have any plans for this afternoon?" "I might go to south Dallas and visit some family members, or go to the cafe my sister manages." Wayne said, "I really wish you wouldn't range over there by yourself." "But some of my family lives there." "When are you coming back? I get off work at 11:00 p.m., and I want to come and pick you up after that." "That sounds great." "What address will you be at?" I gave him the address. "I'll be there no later than 11:45 p.m., so be sure to be at that address." "I will wait for you right there. See you then!" "Do you need any money?" "No, thanks." "Here, take

$50.00 Denise, put the money in your pocket and make sure you eat, all right? I'll see you when I leave work." He gave me a kiss and drove away.

When he arrived at work, some of his homeboys teased him about me. His best friend, Joe Smith, who was also the nephew of the fish place's owner, said, "Hey, man. What's going on with you and Denise?" Wayne replied, "Shit, man, I think I'm really into her." Joe commented that I was awfully young. Wayne admitted, "I know, that's what's got me going, but hell, she not like the rest of those crazy ass women."

Joe smiled and said, "Boy, I think you done got deep. You're going to be all right." Wayne said "Yeah, man, I just never met anyone like her. That shit tripping me out." Joe laughed. "You got girls everywhere." Wayne said, "I'm not worried about that, man. I want a good relationship with her, man, but we both young. Man, I'm almost 19 years old, no kids and never been married. Denise has no children and has never been married, and she don't have a lot of family support. She cool though. I can talk to her about anything. Hell, we fight a little, but she don't be starting shit, man."

Joe said, "If you like that, make her your girl, dude." "As far as I'm concerned, Denise is my girl. My Mom feels good about her, and I don't take women to my t-jones house. Man, you know that. I keep them hoods in the streets." Joe encouraged him to make it work. "She seems like a good girl, man." "I think so, but she was to want me to be the special man in her life."

Joe told Wayne, "Man, go get that girl. I got you. Let me know what you need." Wayne said, "Okay, I may, dude, that's what's up. This is a different move for me, because I don't slow down for no damn woman." Joe laughed. "Man, take your ass to work. It's all good." As he was leaving, Wayne said, "You right, I will. Holla at you later."

Wayne headed back to work, with me on his mind. For a moment, he considered how old I was, how I had never lived life and that I was struggling to finish school. Wayne considered me immature in relationships and began to think that was an advantage for him, because he could teach me what he wanted from a woman.

I was sitting at my sister's cafe, waiting for Wayne to pick me up, wondering where our relationship would go. My mother would be happy as long as I didn't have to move back into her house. Joyce had told everyone she knew that I was stupid and wouldn't amount to anything in her life, because I was trash.

I thought to myself, "Why do people treat me the way they do? Crying on the inside, it's going to be all right. I just know it. Because I have to keep moving, no matter what may come my way."

Right on time, Wayne picked me up. My friends and family seemed to like him, and they talked for a little while. "Denise, you ready to go? It's getting late." "Yes." After we left, Wayne asked me, "Did you have a good time?" "Yes, I did." "Are you hungry?" "Definitely. Can we go to Whataburger?" After we ate, I said, "Wayne, thank you." "For what?" "For looking after me. I'm not used to that, except from my old boyfriend, Brian." "Look, Denise, you're going to be fine, and we will work this all out together." "I understand."

Chapter Seventeen

My stomach began to knot up like a wad of paper, and I began to feel anxious, as if something were majorly wrong.

After we left Whataburger, we headed to Donnie's house. He wasn't home, and we knew he would be gone for two days. Wayne spent the night with me and we became intimate for the first time. By then, we'd known each other for 11 months.

After this, the two of us became inseparable. Wayne went to work and came home at night to be with me. After a couple of days, Wayne got up and headed for work, and Donnie drove up as he was leaving. Everything seemed cool, but when Donnie came inside and I asked him, "How was your trip?" "Good," he said, but his expression told a different story. "Are you okay?" "I'm all right." "Are you sure?" "Yeah."

I had already taken a bath and dressed, so I caught the bus downtown to go shopping. Staying there most of the day, I was actually enjoying my personal time while hanging out downtown. Lunch was delicious, so I shopped a little more and decided that since I was riding the bus, it was a good time to head home.

The bus finally made it to my street and I walked to the house. As I got closer to the door, I began to feel strange. My stomach began to knot up like a wad of paper and I began to feel anxious, as if something were majorly wrong. I went indoors and Donnie was sitting in the living room, watching television. I didn't say anything, and walked to the back room so I could sit down and think about anything that could possibly have happened to upset Donnie.

I finally went to the living room. "Donnie, what is going on with you?" "I don't like the fact that Wayne stayed at my house the nights I was gone, and when I got home this morning he was leaving. What the hell was that about?" "I'm confused. Before you left, everything was okay that he stayed here because you guys are close, and you had told him, 'I don't mind you checking on my cousin, Denise.' Your words, Donnie."

"I may have forgotten that I said that, but I don't want Wayne back at my house anymore, and I mean it!" "So, the man I care for is not welcome where I am staying. Is that what you're saying, Donnie?" He was quiet as I continued. "Because if that's what you mean, then I need to do something different. Wayne is my boyfriend and I am not going to be somewhere he's not welcome. And remember, I pay rent here. I love you, but it's just not right. All of a sudden, things changed." "Are you serious?" Donnie angrily shot back. "This is my house, and I don't have to explain nothing to no one."

"No, that's not true. When people were giving you their money, yes, you should give an explanation to the shit." "You're talking shit." "Hell no, I'm talking facts." "Well, you know what you can do, don't you?" I was angry. "No, what is that, Donnie?" "Move out!" "Okay, no problem, I'll go find another place tomorrow."

I called Wayne and asked him to come get me in the morning, so I could find a new place to live. "What's happening, baby?" I said, "Donnie is over here tripping because you stayed at the house with me for two nights, but it really doesn't matter, because I'm getting tired of everyone's bullshit. Can you pick me up?" Wayne said "Baby, get your things together, I'm leaving work right now." "I'll be waiting."

I was sitting on my bed half-asleep when I was suddenly awakened by Donnie standing over me. He was drunk. "You not going nowhere, you going to give me some of that pussy. Hell, yeah.

Wayne getting it, our other cousin raped you and got it. I'm going to get a little too." I wasn't feeling sleepy any more. "You're my cousin. What the hell, are you crazy?" "No, far from it, but you're going to give me some ass or get out of my house!"

"Well, I guess I'm going to get out of your house because the ass what get got isn't yours, cuz. It's best I get away from you as soon as possible." At that moment, Wayne drove up and got out of the car. He called out to me, "Denise, let's go now before I go off on this clown. I got you. Let's go!" I said I was ready to go, and he helped me with my possessions. Before we left, Wayne got up in Donnie's face. "Look, Donnie, I thought we was better than that, but I guess not. It don't matter really, don't matter. Denise, let's go."

I picked up my clothes as we left, not sure where I was going, or what Wayne had in his mind. He asked me to move in with him at his mother's house, staying with his mother because she often had epileptic seizures, and his two brothers had issues. One was in prison, while the other was addicted to cocaine and would steal things from his mother's home. Wayne was the youngest, and although he had moved out twice, he had always moved back to care for his mother. Wayne had never been to jail for anything but a traffic ticket before I met him, although he sometimes drank alcohol and smoked marijuana.

"Where are you taking me, Wayne?"
"Listen, Denise. I love you and I want to know if you would come and stay with me at my mother's house. We've never did a lot of talking about why I stay with my mother, but it's because she has epileptic seizures often, and I'm the only child she has out of three boys who stays there to take care of her without leaving for days.

I'm there in case the ambulance is called and paramedics have to rush my mother to the hospital. I'm just saying, Denise, you're welcome to be where I am. I really love you."

I didn't know what to say. Finally, I asked, "How do you know your mother will like me? What if she don't want me to stay there after she finds out about all my faults and past experiences?" "Denise, will you stop it? My mother loves God first, and even though I'm not in church like my Mama had me all my life, I still understand what she stands for. Denise, I don't want you out on these streets. I'm not perfect, but I love you, so let's at least go and talk to her."

I agreed, so we headed to Mrs. Alice's house to talk about living with them. I was nervous as we drove up to the apartment complex in Dallas. As I got out of the car, Wayne grabbed my hand, kissed my forehead and said, "It's going to be all right, Denise." I nodded at him, and we entered his mother's apartment.

Chapter Eighteen

After we had been living with his mother for two weeks, Wayne proposed. He took me to a restaurant and gave me a beautiful diamond ring with an 18-karat gold band.

Minister Alice was sitting in her usual place, in a recliner, and greeted us both. "Hello, you two. How are you?" Wayne answered, "Mama, this is Denise, who you actually met last time I came over. Remember, Mama?" "Boy, I remember who she is." I said, "Hello, Mrs. Alice. How are you?" "I'm blessed and doing fine, thank you." She wasted no time getting to the point.

"Young lady, now I understand Wayne wants you to stay here with us because he loves you for once, and you need a place to live. I understand you've been staying with your cousin, Donnie." "Yes, ma'am, and it was all cool with him until I allowed Wayne to stay at the house for the two nights that Donnie was out of town."

Alice thought for a moment, and replied, "Well, if he didn't want Wayne in his house while he was gone, then Wayne shouldn't have been there."

"No, Mrs. Alice, my cousin has never had a problem with Wayne coming over to his house. Before I moved in, Wayne would spend the night and go to Donnie's house without him being there. Truth be told, my cousin had gotten used to us being there. I think my cousin started to have some type of emotions for me he couldn't control. I never dressed provocatively around the house or sexually played with my cousin. So, he became angry because he told me since I'm sleeping with Wayne, I would have to give him some of that ... well, you know." "So, you and Wayne are sleeping together?"

Wayne interrupted. "Mama, what does that have to do with you?" "What do you mean? First of all, I am your mother. Second, I'm a woman of God. And lastly, if you love this young lady, you need to marry her, because you're not going to just be laying up in my house like that. And Denise may get pregnant at some point."

"I got that, Mama. I want to ask her to marry me. I love her, Mama. I'm 18 1/2, almost 19 years old, and I understand you make the decisions in this house since Daddy been deceased. I miss him at times because of you, but I didn't like some of the things he did to you." "I realize that, son, and this is not the time for that conversation."

Wayne continued. "Mama, I'm going to marry Denise if she will have me. I'm going to share that story with her and probably my children." "Be careful, because you are a lot like your father."

It was time for me to clarify things. "To answer your question, Mrs. Alice, yes, I am sleeping with your son. I know we are not married, as you said. I didn't know that was so important when you love someone. It shouldn't matter, as long as you're together. That's how I have always been taught." "Honey, I can tell you're not aware, but nothing becomes binding until you sign it."

I told her I didn't understand. "You and Wayne can have all the sex you desire, but what legally makes you one mind, body and unit is marriage. Because then you are his wife and he becomes your husband."

Wayne insisted that I shouldn't have to rush to marry him because he would be ready when I was. Alice said that I could stay there in their apartment, but we couldn't sleep in the same bedroom until we were married. "Know I go to church during the week and on Sundays, and you are welcome to attend. I would actually love for you to meet my pastor and come by the church. You may enjoy it. Have you done anything in church?" "Not really." "Can you sing or play an instrument?" "I can sing a little bit, but I definitely can't play any musical instrument. I honestly don't even know God like that, but yes, one day I will go to church with you."

Wayne said, "Mama, let's get back to Denise's living arrangements. That's why we're here." Mrs. Alice disagreed. "No, everything I just mentioned is why Denise needs to be here young man, and stop trying to tell me what to talk about in my house."

I said, "Everything is fine, and I understand everything you said, Mrs. Alice. I will help around here wherever I'm needed. Cooking, cleaning, washing and more. I really appreciate you letting me live here, Mrs. Alice." "Okay, no problem. Now, here are the rules: no drugs, no smoking and no bringing a bunch of company in and out of my house, because you never know how people are thinking. And no drinking." "Are we understood?" "Yes, ma'am."

"Mama, are you through preaching now?" "No,

I'm not. Boy, you better be careful. Denise, you can sleep in Wayne's room, and Wayne you sleep in the living room. I don't want you two in the same bedroom together. Do you understand that?" We both said that we did.

"Denise, are you in school now?" "Yes, ma'am, but I'm not doing well, because I've had such unstable living arrangements, Mrs. Alice. And I've been raped all my life by family members, men who were supposed to protect me, and those who were supposed to love me."

Mrs. Alice looked upset. "Let's pray right now, that God moves the hindrances out of your life, and helps you stable your mind, in the name of Jesus. I bind any demonic spirits from this young lady's life. Give her the strength to forgive and forget past hurt and pain that others have caused in her life. And God, I ask you to forgive those who trespassed against Denise, and help her to let go and let God heal and deliver her in righteousness. Remember the sick and the shut-ins all over this nation as we leave this place and we are never from your presence. In Jesus' name, amen."

I said, "Thank you for that. I will learn soon how to operate in God, Mrs. Alice. When I'm ready, will you be here?" "Honey, you are a vessel of God and it is my duty for any soul who desires help to be on my post, and to pray for those who are lost." "You are a really nice person, Mrs. Alice, and thank you for praying for me and everyone else." "You are a great person, Denise. Don't let the enemy use you." "Thank you, Mrs. Alice."

Wayne and I went to his car and began unloading my clothes to take inside. I was so happy, never knowing I would be preparing for some trials that would one day allow the greatest blessing upon me. I told Wayne, "I'm so excited, and I want us to have a happy life with children of our own, Wayne. A boy and a girl. Wouldn't that be nice?" "Denise, that would be great. We have things to get together first, because I do want to marry you, Denise."

After we had been living with his mother for two weeks, Wayne proposed. He took me to a restaurant and gave me a beautiful diamond ring with an 18-karat gold band. Wayne said, "I never thought anyone would ever have meant this much to me. Denise, you are so beautiful to me, with a warm heart when it comes to anyone. I realize you've had it really hard this far, being mistreated, and I'm sorry that happened to you. But I want you to know that I'm not perfect, and it's possible I may never be, because I believe I may have inherited some of my father's ways. But will do all I can to do good by you. I've never had a wife and you've never had a husband.

"I ask you in the presence of friends and family who you didn't know was here (he laughed a bit), would you marry me, Denise Brown, and be my wife?" I felt stiff and tense, as though I was making a mistake. However, I managed to bypass these feelings of something being completely wrong. "Yes, Wayne, I will marry you." I began to feel sick to my stomach. Wayne said excitedly, "Y'all here, this beautiful lady, she is going to marry me." After hearing this, everyone began to clap for us, giving us a hug and offering congratulations.

A week later, we went downtown to the Dallas Records Building to see what was needed to get a marriage license. The young lady at the counter asked us how old we were. "I'm 15 years old." "And you, young man?" Wayne said that he was 18 1/2, and his birthday was coming soon. The clerk told Wayne everything was fine, and asked him his name. "Wayne, you are old enough to sign your own papers." Then she turned to me. "Young lady, where are your parents?" I admitted that I wasn't sure. "I haven't seen my mother in about two years." The clerk said "Well, you will have to get a guardian to sign for you to be married. You can come back then with your Social Security card and another identification card, along with an adult to sign for you. I apologize."

As we walked away, I said to Wayne, "This is crap. I don't want to talk to Joyce at all." "Let's just try, Denise. Maybe she will just sign the papers without any hassle." I thought about it a minute. "Okay, Wayne, I really don't want to go over there to her house, but I will do it for us."

Chapter Nineteen

Lisa said, "Why are you so upset, Wayne, if I mean nothing to you?" Wayne told her she had to go. "I don't have time for all this right now."

It wasn't just that I didn't want to see my mother, but I was trying to deal with both situations, dealing with my mother and getting married. I first thought to myself, "No, find your father." I really didn't understand the first thought. After running back downtown just to find out that I needed a parent's permission to get married at 15 years old, I was missing the fact that I was still a minor according to the law. The only saving grace for Wayne at 18 1/2 sleeping with a 15-year old is to prove good intent to be married to me, so he would not be charged with rape.

Wayne interrupted my train of thought by asking me, "Are you hungry, baby? Can I take you somewhere?" "Yes, maybe you should get food for me and your mother, that way we won't have to cook. Okay?" "That's fine. What do you want?" "How about some fish from the fish place?" "No problem. I'm going to stop now, and that way I can let them know that I might also be a little late."

I watched Wayne go into where he originally worked to get us food to share. It seemed like he was in there for about 30 minutes. Wayne was unaware that a woman he had dated for years was a new hire at this location. Wayne said, "Hello, what are you doing at my store? And why you back now to come here, Lisa?" "I never stopped loving you, and I didn't know you worked here." Wayne snorted. "Bullshit, and you know it." "I want my man back again.".

"Are you crazy, woman? I think you know I have moved on, and I'm getting ready to get married." Lisa laughed. "To that kid? You and I both know she can't do nothing for you, Wayne." "No, that's where you're wrong because you're 32 years old and she's younger. That makes her nothing?" Lisa said, "No, Wayne, it makes you seem desperate for a younger female, when you have 32 years of experience in your bed. I think taught you well. And I work, baby, and I took care of your every need, where your little friend has to learn how to be a woman. While we're on the subject of marriage ..." Wayne cut her off mid-sentence. "We are not on the subject matter of marriage regarding you and I, and far as my future is concerned, that's none of your business."

"Why are you so upset, Wayne, if I mean nothing to you?" "You have to go. I don't have time for all this right now." He headed back to the car to bring the food for his mother and me. As he opened the door, he didn't say much. Eventually, I asked, "Wayne, are you okay?" "Yeah, why do you ask?" "Because you were smiling when you go out of the car but when you came back you looked upset. That's all." "I'm good, Denise. I want you to enjoy your food. What are you planning this evening?" "Probably go by Joyce's house and talk with her about signing the marriage papers."

"How do you think that will go?" "To be honest, I really don't know. Maybe Joyce will be happy, because she won't have to worry about me anymore. I will become your responsibility. Even in school, I feel so wired about everything in my life." "What do you mean? You don't want to marry me?" I told him the truth. "Not really, it's just that I have a feeling that something could go so wrong."

"Let's not think like that and keep going. Denise, no one said everything is going to be easy." "You're right, and you better go to work, because you're already late, and you'll be even later if you don't leave right now." We agreed to talk later, and affirmed our love for each other, and then he left.

Wayne was dreading arriving at work, because Lisa worked there now, and he expected her to try and cause problems with Denise at some point, as she was very dominating. When Lisa wanted something, she wouldn't stop until she got it.

Arriving at work, he noticed Joe was there working to help the store out because it was a lot busier than the other location in the central part of Dallas. Joe walked over to Wayne and said, "Hey man, what's going on?" "Nothing much, man, what's up with you?" "The work. Hey man, I heard about what went down with Denise and Donnie. That fool said he put his cousin out because she was coming in too late." "Man, you believe that bull? This dude got mad because he was out of town, and Denise allowed me to spend the night with her. This clown told me before he left that it was cool to stay over there and look out for his cousin. The problem was that he didn't want me to sleep with her."

"Dude, damn, I won't lie. I didn't think you would get that no way." He laughed. "Just messing with you, bro, so why you think that clown put her out, man?" "This fool was pushing up on his own cousin, man." Joe looked surprised. "You lying?" Wayne said, "This man told Denise you giving him some ass, you might as well give me some too. He was drunk, but that's no excuse, man." "I feel ya, that's crazy. So, when's the wedding?" "Denise gotta get her old lady to sign the papers, because she's only 15." Joe said, "So, that's what's up!" "Let's both get to work, okay? We can shop it up later on." Joe agreed.

Wayne went to work, trying his best to ignore Lisa. He was thinking about me and if I were okay, while I was on my way to talk to my mother, after two years of not seeing or speaking to her. About 5:15 p.m., I arrived at Joyce's house in south Dallas and knocked on the door. I had a calm spirit when she opened the door, and she seemed genuinely glad to see me. "What do you want, Denise?" "Hello, Mama. I came to see you and get you to help me with something." "What do you need help with?" "I met someone who I'm living with, and we want to get married." Joyce seemed surprised. "Get married?" "Yes, I love him and believe me, he loves me, too."

"How old is this guy?" "He's 18 1/2 years old." "That's not bad. When are you trying to get married? As soon as possible?" "Yes, all we need now is our marriage license." "Okay, let's do it next week." "That's fine, Mama. I'll bring Wayne to meet you." "I said you wasn't going to amount to anything, but look at you, trying to be somebody's wife. I got to tell your sisters about that. Lenise ran off somewhere. I haven't seen her and I thought she was with you." "No, I haven't seen her, but I'll look out for her." "Lenise just up and left school one day and disappeared. Just like that!" "Did you report her missing to the police?" "Hell no, she knows where she lives." "Mama, she's still a minor." Her demeanor changed. "Hell, you was and still is a minor, but I'm not looking for you, am I?" "I guess not."

Joyce asked, "You have any money on you, so Mama can buy something to eat?" I gave her $30, and she said, "Thank you, I need this little change." "Mama, I'm getting ready to go to the house. I will talk with you later."

After I left, she walked around the corner to tell her friend Linda that I had given her $30, and that I had asked her to sign some papers for marriage. "Are you gonna sign the papers?" "Hell yeah, let whoever he is have that headache shit, she's already out there anyway. "Joyce, that girl ain't nothing but 15 years old. Does she have any children?" "I don't think so. I didn't ask." Linda was surprised. "Really?" "I was half-drunk, and, well, them her kids if she has any." "You can't think like that. Denise is a pretty good kid." "That's what you think. I glad she gone. She was always talking about my friends, saying they was looking at her, and said when they come to visit me they often had sex with her. And girl, check this out. Denise told me my cousin touched her when she was little, about the age of 11 years. She didn't say it she just pointed at her private area."

"Did you take Denise to the doctor?" "No, she was lying and I told her to shut her mouth and don't be talking out of my auntie's house." Linda was upset. "She was a baby. How do you know she was lying, Joyce?" "Because my auntie didn't play that mess at her house." Linda persisted. "Joyce, I'm just saying all children don't make up stories." She continued. "Joyce, I can't tell you how to raise your kid but you put that girl down all the time. She seems to be a good child that might go bad at any time." "If she does, that's on her, because I'm not coming to get her out of jail. I don't have no money for that and I have two kids at home." Linda replied, "Correction, one kid. Because Lenise is gone wherever the hell she wants to be at 15 years old." Joyce was so angry that she stopped speaking to Linda for three weeks. But Linda didn't mind, because she knew she was telling her right.

Chapter Twenty

"My name is Lisa, and I want to know why are you living in my man's and future mother in law's house."

I found Mrs. Alice back at the house, praying. She could feel I was upset. How are you today, Denise?" "Okay. I've just had a long day." "God loves you. Maybe you should go and get some rest." "Maybe I should. Has Wayne called yet?" "Get some rest, and I will wake you as soon as your sweetie-pie calls." I laughed. "Okay, Mrs. Alice."

Two hours later Wayne called to check on us. "Hey, Mama, how you doing, old lady?" "I'm doing great son, and you?" "I'm fine. Did Denise make it back home?" "Yes, she is here, but she's asleep right now." "Don't wake her up, Mama." "No, I told her I would wake you when you called." Alice called out to me, telling me that Wayne was on the telephone. "Hey baby, how are you doing?" I said, "Better, now that I hear your voice." "Is everything okay?" "Yeah, I guess so. Joyce is going to sign the papers next week so that we can get married."

Wayne said, "That's good news, right?" "Just you, Wayne." "I'll be home soon. I just wanted to be sure you are all right." "Yes, I'm fine. Get back to work before we both be looking for a job." I laughed, and continued. "It's good hearing your voice, Wayne." "I'm glad you miss me, future Mrs. Henderson. I'll talk to you later, okay?"

After Wayne hung up, the manager requested that he take some product to another store, and since Lisa was training to be an assistant manager, the manager wanted her to go along with him. After they both got into the van and started down the street, Lisa said, "You're coming back home, Wayne. You didn't have to leave me the first time. You are the one had all the women around the club. You ran between me and the ballroom. All of you guys had more women than you could handle, then you would leave for two weeks at a time before coming home." Wayne said, "Then if I were that bad you shouldn't want me at your house. Now shut the fuck up talking to me and ride, because you're getting on my damn nerves."

Lisa wasn't giving up. "You don't mean nothing you're saying, because you know any time you want me, I'm going to be there for you. That's why you been treating me like that for 2 1/2 years." Wayne said, "Look, you tied up with a young dude, and I'm not your damn kid, and I suggest you respect what I do. And as far as you getting this in my pants, you ain't never going to be a regular, because her name is Denise. Only thing you can do for me is open that ass when I can't get none and another girl fired my ass. That's what's up." Lisa said, "You know, I buy you anything you want, Wayne." "See, that's where you're wrong. I'm a package deal. My woman is at home with my Mama. Know I'm done with all this shit!"

By now they had arrived at the other location of the fish place. Lisa and Wayne unloaded the product and took it into the building. They didn't talk for a while. After an hour and a half, they returned to the van and drove to the fish place in south Dallas. They got out and went to work. Two hours later, Lisa went to the ballroom near Alice's house, since she knew where she stayed. Lisa had a few drinks and drove past the house. Later, Wayne drove up, sat in his car and thought about all he had going on, and the move of marriage, assuring himself that he was ready for the one woman he had ever really loved. Of course, Wayne was young himself, with quite a bit of experience already when it came to women and street life.

He got out of the car and went into the house to find me on the phone. Someone had just called before he walked in and asked for me. "Yes, this is Denise. How can I help you?" "My name is Lisa, and I want to know why are you living in my man's and future mother in law's house." I said, "What, are you crazy?" "No, bitch, I'm not crazy. But you better leave Wayne alone or you're going to have some problems. Because he just moved out of our house because he likes doing what he wants to do, but he can screw me anytime he want to and he can come home. Don't get it twisted home, girl."

Wayne asked who was on the phone. I said, "I don't know, but she says her name is Lisa, and you just moved out of your house together, and you can have sex with her whenever you want. And you can always come back home. Is that right?" Wayne grabbed the phone, and I asked him, "Why the hell you calling her?" Lisa answered the phone and said, "I already told you, Wayne, you coming back home. I'm not playing." Wayne spoke quietly. "I'm trying not to disrespect you in my mother's house. Don't call back here no more." He hung up and followed me to a room at the back of the apartment, desperate to explain what had just happened.

"Lisa was an ex-girlfriend, and when I went out earlier today to get you and Mama's food, she was behind the counter. I asked her what she was doing there, and she said she worked there now. I shared with her that I'm done and my woman is at home. Baby, she means nothing to me." I said, "I'm fine, Wayne. I'm good, and honestly, I really don't feel like talking about all of this. Because it's foolish and totally not worth the conversation. I'm going out."

Wayne said "Denise, listen, please." "Wayne you're fine. I love you. I'll be back later. I just need some time to think." "Let's talk about

159

this now, as I don't want to do this daily, Denise."
"I don't understand what I need to talk about--what
you told me, of course. After your dealing with
this stupid woman today, you could have already
told me about her, Wayne. Because we had nights
where all we did was talk about our struggles. I'm
doing better Wayne, just give me a minute to get
some alone time. That's all I'm asking."

Wayne finally said, "Okay, I don't like it,
but okay. Am I going to have to find you?" "No,
I'm fine. I'll see you later." "Where are you
going?" "I'm going to my family's house, where
you picked me up the other day." "Can I drop you
off?" "I'd rather ride the bus." "I don't want you
riding the bus." "Okay, that's fine. Can we go
now?" "Okay, do you have money for food?"
"Yes." "I want you to take my money and save
yours up, baby. I really don't want you to stay a
couple of days. Why can't you stay for a little
while? I don't want you to spend the night away

from me." I said, "I'm not being away from you. I'm allowing you to fix all this. Wayne, I've been through a lot, but you already know that, baby." "Okay, Denise. Just come back home tonight."

"Okay, just let me hang out a bit." "Can I come later and pick you up?" "I can get a ride home." "Denise, I need to come and get you." "That's fine. I'll see you later tonight."

He gave me a kiss on the forehead, and told me he loved me. Looking back at him as I went into the house, I could tell there was a lot going through his mind. Wayne was thinking of the love he had for me, where he wanted to be, and how there were things in his life that he'd failed to share with me during the long journey in our relationship. This included affairs, addictions, murders and more.

Wayne went back to his job to talk to Joe about what was going on. "Hey Joe, what's up, man?" "You all right, man? What's happening?"

Wayne said, "Man, you remember that chick Lisa I was living with?" "Yeah, what's up?" "Man, she's working here." Joe looked surprised. "How the hell did that happen?" "Man, I don't know. I had Denise in the car when I came up here to get her and Mama something to eat. This broad follows me through the store talking about how I'm coming back home because she did nothing wrong. I left her because I had other women, man. After work, she went to the ballroom around the corner of my house, drove by and later called Denise. She told her who she was and her plan to get me back."

Joe said, "What the hell? So, what are you going to do? This chick is bad news, man." "I want her fired from this fish place, man, because I don't want to go bad." "You know we can't fire her unless she does something unethical. That would allow us to get rid of her." Wayne sighed. "Yeah, I know, man." "Just find a way to deal with it. Try not to deal with her when you don't have to." "All right, man. you right. I am going to have to tell these broads what's going on, because some of them are still calling the house and I haven't talked to them. Mama let me know they called." Joe said, "Man, do you want Denise? Because if you do, you're going to have to slow down." "Man, for real. Do you remember how many girls you have?" "Hell no, so you have a point." He laughed. "Say, man, go get your girl and be good to her. Tell her the truth, all right?" "Break the code, man." Joe laughed. "All right, dude." "Later, man. I'm going to get my baby." "Take care, man."

Wayne sat in his car for a minute, then drove to get me. About 11:30 p.m., Wayne arrived at my family's home to pick me up. I was standing outside, talking to two girls, who said they were checking on me. Little did I know that when Brian died, his daughters--Janet and Patricia--were selling more dope than they made, and when they gave me the money, they were trying to tie me up in the dope game without telling me. I knew nothing about Brian selling dope until the FBI busted the dope house.

At this point, I thought nothing of it, and continued to try and move on with my life. But Brian's daughters asked me to meet them one night at a club to hang out. I asked them, "How have you two been?" Janet said, "We've been good, Denise, but we haven't heard from you in a while." "Okay, I guess. Just taking life one day at a time right now." Patricia asked, "So, are you going to be able to meet us at the club Saturday, so we can sit and talk about all the good times you two had? We just need to talk." "Okay, I can do that. I'm sure I'm not doing anything that night." Janet said, "That's great! I'm looking forward to seeing you. Why don't you wear black? That's what we're all wearing." "Why black?" Janet laughed. "Because it makes me look smaller." "Okay, black it is.

That's strange, but okay." I saw Wayne waiting for me in the car. "Look, I have to go. I'll see you guys then, okay?"

Janet and Patricia believed that I had something to do with their father going to jail for drugs, guns and raping minors, but the truth is that I never spoke to anyone about it. I didn't know much, because Brian shielded me from knowing very much. The feds were close to getting these girls, and the girls didn't want me to somehow talk to them and get them convicted. So, they planned to murder me by luring me to a busy club where people would not be paying a lot of attention to certain violent activities. The dark conspiracy included Carry Woodall, the club owner, and a close friend of Brian.

I got into the car. "Hi, Wayne." "Hey, baby, you all right?" "Yeah…can we just go home?" "Okay. I'm cool with that." We went home, and Alice had gone to church, after which she was going to her mother's house. We had to the house to ourselves. Wayne said, "Come here, Denise. Listen, I love you. That's all that matters, okay? Don't ever make me feel like you're leaving me because I can't deal with that."

I told him I understood and that I loved him. Wayne said, "Let's shower and go to bed." We showered together, became intimate and went to bed. We slept peacefully and enjoyed our night. The next day, Wayne got up, kissed me and left for work. I woke up about 9:30 a.m. to another call from Lisa. "This is Lisa. I want your man." "Look, you work with him. What are you calling me for? Go tell him and stop calling here. You're interrupting my beauty rest. Goodbye, clown!" I hung up.

Chapter Twenty-One

Janet and another girl drew a gun and said, "She's going with us." Cathy said, "I don't know about that." Patricia said, "What are you going to do?" Janet said, "Let's get this bitch out of here."

Two days later, I was planning to meet Janet and Patricia at the club that night, unaware of their evil plans. Wayne was at work and had to stay late, because he needed to go to the ballroom to help with a major concert. I told Wayne I was going out with some people I know.

"Denise, what time are you leaving?" "8:30 p.m." "How are you getting there?" "I'm riding with my friend, Cathy Cloud, and then staying at Barbra's house." Wayne was quiet for a second. "Are you sure you're going to be okay, Denise?" "Yes." "Are you sure?" "Yes, Wayne, everything is going to be fine."

As I was getting dressed, I walked through the living room where Mrs. Alice sat in her recliner. Looking directly at me, she asked, "Where are you going? Ain't nothing out there in those streets." "I know, I'm just going to hang out with a few people." "No, those people are not good for you to be hanging with." "Why not?" "Because God gave me a lot of things. You are special, and the devil desires to use you." "I'll keep that in mind," I said, as I prepared to leave.

Mrs. Alice said, "Come here and let me pray over you." When she was finished, she said, "Denise, I'll see you when you return." "Good night, Mrs. Alice."

When I got to the club, something didn't feel right. Cathy, whom I knew from my nights at the club, asked me where I'd be sitting as I exited her car. I told her I had to go to the restroom first, then I was going to sit up in the middle section with Brian's daughters. "What are their names?"

"Janet and Patricia Brown." "Hmm, those names sound familiar. I've been on these streets a long time, and I know when something doesn't seem right at all, Denise." "I don't know, Cathy. I did feel strange when I got to the front door. I'm going on out here, okay?" "Are you sure, honey?" "Yeah, I'm good. Come on up when you finish."

I walked upstairs and sat down with the two gangsters, Janet and Patricia. Janet said, "Hello. Order you something to drink? We got you, okay?" I ordered a strawberry wine cooler. Patricia asked the waitress to add the drink to their tab after it arrived.

A few minutes after I began to drink, I began to feel sick to my stomach, and this time I began to cramp, feeling totally weird. Janet and Patricia offered to take me home. Cathy said "Hell, no. She came to the club with me." Janet and Patricia both drew a gun and said, "She's going with us." Cathy said, "I don't know about that."

Patricia said, "What are you going to do?" Janet said, "Let's get this bitch out of here."

Because Cathy hadn't felt right about the situation, she had called my cousins and friends who were part of gang activities and other organizations, and they were all standing around the front and back doors of the club. When I reached the exit, three guys told Janet and Patricia to let me go. They all had machine guns, so they were able to walk me to the car. Guess who got out of the car? Wayne, Joe, Donnie and some other guys I didn't know.

I passed out, and Wayne took me to the hospital, because the people behind the bar at the club had slipped something in my drink. I stayed in the hospital three days until the GHB date rape drug was out of my system. Wayne was pissed off, because he didn't understand what was going on until I told him that before we met, I dated another man who had raped me from when I was

12 years old to when I was 14 years old, along with other girls.

"Wayne, the evening you picked me up after Lisa's phone call, the young ladies who were talking to me in the yard were Brian's daughters. He was murdered in prison, and the girls thought I had something to do with him being in jail. But I knew nothing about this, because I went to the runaway center. That's where I was taken and I couldn't even see him, because the judge and District Attorney's office did not allow it. I was a minor, so that's all that was. Wayne, I apologize and thank you for being there."

Wayne said, "Denise, that was my job. I'm pissed because you didn't tell me who you were meeting at the club." "I know, I thought my heart was in the right place but I guess I was wrong. I almost died, and possibly some other people could have died, too. I'm so sorry." "This can't happen no more. You're going to be my wife and I need to know where you are. If you can't do what I ask you, then we can do something different, because I'm not putting up with all that. If Cathy hadn't called me, you could have been gone. Denise, are you listening?" "Yes, yes, it won't happen again." "I'll be back later on. I have to work the ballroom tonight." "Can I go with you?" "No, you need to stay home and get some rest."

Chapter Twenty-Two

As soon as I began walking back to the house, I saw Wayne drive up with some girl in a BMW. They kissed and hugged before they got out of the car.

I stayed asleep for about five hours and woke up about 5:00 a.m., realizing that Wayne hadn't come home. I couldn't sleep and 8:00 a.m. came, with Wayne still not home. About 3:00 p.m., Wayne finally came home, took a bath and lay down without an explanation. When I woke him up to talk, he started getting upset, so I left him alone. Wayne woke up about 6:45 p.m., went into the kitchen and cooked some steaks. He didn't have much to say so I went into the other room and watched television.

At around 10:00 p.m., Wayne got dressed and said he had to work the ballroom that night again. I didn't say anything. When 3:30 a.m. came and Wayne was still not home, I got up and walked to the ballroom. Seeing Joe there, I asked him if he'd seen Wayne. He said that Wayne had left to take some things out to the owner's house. "Why is his car sitting out in the parking lot?" "He's in one of the company vehicles."

As soon as I began walking back to the house, I saw Wayne drive up with some girl in a BMW. They kissed and hugged before they got out of the car. She asked eagerly, "Can I see you tomorrow?" "Yes, I'll call you." As she drove away, she said, "Okay, I'll be waiting."

Wayne turned and saw me standing there. All I could think of was about how people had treated me over the years, and I became angry. Glaring at Wayne, I demanded answers. "Now we're dating other people without sharing the information?" Wayne asked, "What the hell you doing around here this time of the morning?" I said, "I thought I had a man, a future husband. But I guess I was wrong. But don't worry, I'm headed to the house." "Okay, I'll be there." Joe muttered, "Man, you are so going to get your head busted being so stupid. What's wrong with you? I told you that if you don't want that young lady, let her go about her business." "I love Denise. Man, I'm just tripping." "Man, you've been smoking and drinking a little bit. That hard alcohol?" Wayne said he'd had brandy, gin and a few other things you can't drink. "I'm a good man. I'm going home. I'll holla at you tomorrow."

Wayne walked in the house, not keeping in mind that I was still a 15-year old. "What's your problem?" I didn't hesitate to reply. "You seeing other women." "What's the problem, they're just my friends." "You kiss your friends and sleep with them?" "Shut the hell up." "You shut the hell up." As he walked to the bedroom I was in, he became belligerent. "What the hell you say?" Immediately, he slapped me so hard that the right side of my face swelled up. "You're not going to be hitting me." I hit Wayne with an iron, and kept hitting him while crying, "What's wrong with you, Wayne?" He asked me if I were crazy, and hit me again.

The stress had me in a rage, as I picked up objects from the home to hurt Wayne and his brother, William, who ran into the room and stopped the fight. I was bleeding, and Wayne had a cut on the side of his arm from a bottle. Wayne asked William, "Man, what do you want?" "Say dude, you don't be hitting on no woman. What the hell is wrong with you? And you two fighting in Mama's house." I said, "I can move out. He hit me and I got him off me." Mrs. Alice was now awake. "What's going on in here?" she asked. I said, "Ask your son, he hit me for no reason. I'm going to get my things and move out." Wayne said, "Man, it wasn't like that."

William said, "Like what, man? You better keep your hands off any woman. You have a mother and no sister or daughter, but if you did, you're not going to want people or any man putting their hands on them. Come on, you know better." Wayne said, "That's my girl." "That doesn't make any difference." Wayne said, "No, let her stay here, I'm leaving." Mrs. Alice said, "Wayne, you know better. Look at that girl." Wayne looked at me. "I'm sorry, Denise. I'm gone." I was crying, "I can't do all this at 15 years old or at any age."

I continued to cry, and couldn't attend school for a week until my eye cleared up. I decided that weekend to go and spend the night with Cathy. "Cathy, are you busy?" "Hey, Denise. Is everything okay?" "Not really." "Can I come and visit you for a few days?" "Sure, come on." I packed some of my things and left for four days, never telling anyone where I was.

When I got to Cathy's house, I told her that I had had a fight with Wayne. "What was it about?" "He was drunk, and I asked a lot of questions, and he got mad and hit me, and I hit him back with a bottle and cut his arm." "Girl, you too young for all this. Denise, why don't you go home to your mother?" "Because she don't want me at her house, just my brother Anthony and my twin sister Lenise. She worships the ground they walk on, and besides, I would only have to clean and wait on all three of them like a maid. I'm not willing to do no more of that. I'm tired, Cathy." "Where is your Dad?" "He's driving a truck for Mayflower and is never around. "Try to get in touch with someone, please, and of course, you can stay here, but you have to stay in school without missing so much. Look, do you want to be with Wayne?" "Yes, because I love him, Cathy. He hasn't been acting like he loves me lately." "Do you truly know what love is?" "I think so. All I know is that my heart feels heavy when he's not around, or I don't know where he is." "Baby, I'll be honest. Wayne had some issues long before you came along. He is a good guy, but he's drinking more. Denise, I don't know if he's doing drugs, but some time will tell that story. Hold on, someone's knocking at the door."

She went to the door. "Who is it?" I could hear Wayne on the other side of the door. "Can I talk to Denise?" "That's up to her." "Yeah. I'm not going to bring problems to your house." I gathered up my things. "I'll see you later, okay? Thank you for letting me stay a few days." "I think you should be with family, Denise." "I know. It's okay. I see you later."

Wayne said, "Hi, baby. I miss you, and I'm sorry for touching you. Can we go eat and go home, please? I can't live without you and I want to marry you. I'm on my knees. Please, I'm going to do better." "You hurt me, Wayne." "I'm going to do better. I promise, baby, come home." "Okay."

We left, stopped to pick up some food, and went home. Wayne became more emotional and undressed me, and we were intimate all night.

Chapter Twenty-Three

Someone called the police, and I didn't run. Standing in the middle of the street, I waited for them, as I heard the sirens getting louder and closer.

The next morning, Wayne got up and took me to breakfast before he went to work, and dropped me off at home. "Denise, I love you and you can't ever leave me, because I have never let anyone get this close to me. You're going to be my wife. I'm in love with you and I can't let go. I'm not living without you, Denise." "I love you too, Wayne. I'm not leaving you." "I have to go to work, baby. I'll call you on my break. Call me and let me know if you leave the house, okay?" I said, "Okay. I will."

As I sat and reflected, I thought about how I loved Wayne, but I didn't know if I were in love because I didn't understand all that I got up and cleaned the house and washed clothes until I heard a knock at the door. It was Joyce. She said, "Hey, I came by to see if you'll want to go downtown tomorrow to get your marriage license." I said, "That's fine. I'll let Wayne know. Mama, this is Wayne's mother, Mrs. Alice." Joyce said, "How are you doing? I'm trying to get this one married." Mrs. Alice inquired, "Why? She's just 15 years old." "Honey, she's already been out there. She's going to be all right." "I see it differently, Mrs. Joyce." "Well, what's his name..." I said, "It's Wayne, Mama." "Wayne wants a wife. I'm giving him one. Maybe he can help her, because I can't." I said, "I'll let Wayne know." Joyce said she would see us tomorrow. "About 10:30 a.m. would be good, because I have to be at the WIC office at 2:00 p.m." I said that would be okay, so she left.

Mrs. Alice had been listening to our conversation. "I understand your life even more now, because you have no real family support as a teenager and I don't think that you're going to make it without it." I admitted that she was right. "You want to go to church with me tonight?" "No, but I'll go another time."

Wayne arrived home later that day. "Hey baby, how are you?" "Fine, what about you?" "I'm good." "My Mama came by today, and she wants to meet us tomorrow at 10:30 a.m. to sign the marriage papers." "Okay, that's cool. You happy?" "Yeah…have you eaten? Alice has cooked dinner." "Okay, let's eat. Baby, can a man get a plate of food around here?"

As I fixed his plate, I realized I was nervous about the marriage. But we woke up the next morning and met Joyce at the Courts building, where she finally met Wayne, the man who was marrying her daughter. Although she didn't really care, she just wanted me to be considered grown in the state of Texas. We got the marriage license and waited 30 days before we had our wedding, which we planned to celebrate at the home of Wayne's grandmother, Betty Henderson.

Two weeks before the wedding, Wayne came home late. "Denise, wake up." I woke up and asked him, "What is it?" He took his fist and punched me in the nose. It started bleeding all over everything. "What is wrong with you?" Wayne said, "Sit down. You're not leaving this house. You hear me?" He grabbed me by the hair. "Stop it, Wayne!" Wayne said, "Shit, I'm tired. Go clean yourself up."

There was a knock at the door and, it was the girl in the BMW. Wayne opened the door and said, "What's up girl? Why didn't you call me?" "Because you told me what time to come by your house, Wayne." "Damn, why would I want to do that? My girl is here." "Because you were drunk and high. I'm gone. I don't have time for this bullshit." "Woman, look. I'm not in the mood for your mouth. Get the hell off of my porch, and don't ever come to my house again."

Two weeks later, Mrs. Alice, Joyce, Betty Henderson and his aunties gave us a truly beautiful wedding. Everyone was dressed up and waiting for the ceremony to start. I was still at home with one of my sisters, Barbra. I knew my sister, but hadn't been around her for a long time, so I was sitting at the house, not dressed, and saying I didn't want to get married. Barbra said, "Denise, if you don't want to, don't. But Mama wants you married." "Why? What does it benefit her?" Barbra explained. "She won't have to worry about you going to school and having clothing, food and more. Actually, she told me to push you to marry Wayne." "Who does that to her children? I will never be like her. This man beats on me sometimes, but sometimes he's okay. I don't understand him either." "Well, you need to make your mind up."

"I know, because they keep calling from Betty's house, and the preacher has been waiting a while already." "What is Wayne wearing?" "He's wearing a black suit, white shirt, black tie, black shoes and a black and white pocket decorator." "What are you wearing?" I described it to her. "A black top, white skirt, black stockings and black shoes. And a white flower in my hair." Barbra sat down next to me. "Sis, what do you want?" "Barbra, I love Wayne, but honestly, I don't want to get married." "Then you tell Mama and Wayne."

About 20 minutes after our conversation, Joyce knocked on the door, and I invited her in. "Girl, what are you doing, and why are you not dressed?" "I don't want to get married, Mama." "Girl, please get your ass dressed. Everybody is waiting on you." "Mama, Wayne be fighting on me." She said, "Fight back, girl. I'm not going through all this with you. They paid me to get all this stuff together and I did, and you're not going to mess it up. Let's go. And Barbra, why didn't you make her get dressed while you were sitting here on your ass doing nothing?" "Mama, the girl said she don't want to get married. She's only 15 years old." "That don't mean nothing. Hell, I was married at 16 years old and it didn't kill me. She's going to be all right. Let's go. Denise, get in the car."

I got dressed, and the three of us headed to the wedding, where everyone was waiting to start the service, while fussing at me for being late. We were married, and it was a done deal. Everyone partied all night, and I was so frustrated, but never showed it. Instead, Wayne and I thanked everyone for their support.

As the last guests left, Joyce said, "See, that wasn't so bad. And when Wayne gets upset, go lay him down and make him feel good. You'll be all right. I'll see you later. Make sure you stay over here and not at my house, because I'm not getting involved into y'all's mess." "I will, Mama."

My mother didn't understand what she'd done to me, leaving me with so much anger and rage by pushing me into a place that might hurt me. After Joyce left, Wayne asked me why I had been late for our wedding. "Wayne, I don't know what's going to happen next." "What do you mean?" "I mean, what's happening next in my life, my future, and just how all this will turn out. Wayne, will we stay together? Just questions of my own, baby." "Stop worrying and just live, Denise."

About a month after we were married, Wayne stopped coming home. He showed up a few weeks later, saying nothing about where he'd been. "Hey, baby, what's going on?" I said, "Is that all you have to say to me after leaving me here with your mother for a month? And she's been sick. What's wrong with you, Wayne?" "Don't I help you and take care of you? Why are you all in my ear?" "You're right. Don't worry about it."

Alice called us over. "Look, you two are married. All this fussing and fighting has got to stop because I'm sick, and you say you love each other. You shouldn't be fighting." Wayne said, "Man, I don't want to hear all this. I'm getting ready to leave. I see y'all later." I said, "I'm sorry, Mrs. Alice. You can't talk to Wayne. He's staying out late and having girls coming to the door. I'm going to visit Barbra today at the cafe in south Dallas and talk." Mrs. Alice said, "You shouldn't be hanging around those places, Denise." "I won't be out there too long."

I got dressed and headed out to see Barbra for a little while. I caught the bus to the strip on Oakland Boulevard and went to the cafe. Someone mentioned that Barbra wouldn't come to work until later in the afternoon, and I could wait around, if needed. I said, "Yeah, I'll wait to see her."

As I walked out of the cafe, two girls from the past remembered me from my days of being with Brian. They had sold dope for him and they resented how he had taken care of me with money, cars, drivers, mink coats and more. They thought I never had to do anything but go to school, the beauty shop, restaurants and shopping. Brian had never let anyone touch me.

They approached me and said, "Bitch, we don't like you and we're going to beat your ass." I said, "I'm not bothering anybody, but don't put your hands on me, ever." One of them ran up to me and I hit her, and knocked her through a big wide window in front of the cafe. She lay there, going through so much glass that I thought she had died. The other girl started swinging at me, so I ran into the alley, picked up a beer bottle and cut her up. She survived, but had scars for the rest of her life.

Someone called the police, and I didn't run. Standing in the middle of the street, I waited for them, as I heard the sirens getting louder and closer. They swarmed in from everywhere, it seemed. Several of them pulled their guns and one shouted that I need to put the bottle down. My clothes were soaked with blood, and I was in shock.

The police told me to sit down on the curb and put my hands up, and I complied. I was still just 16 years old, and having a hard time with life. One police officer asked me how old I was, and I said I was 21 years old. After the EMTs assessed my injuries, and made sure I was okay, the police put handcuffs on me. Another officer asked, "Young lady, how old are you?" I repeated that I was 21. Still another officer said, "She's not 21. Well, right now, let's take her to the Lew Sterrett

Justice Center, and put her in a holding cell until her guardians are called."

I called Mrs. Alice collect. "Denise, what are you doing at that jail?" "Two girls jumped me, and I had to defend myself. Is Wayne home?" "He's at the store." "Can you bring my marriage license down here and tell them how old I am, so I can be transferred to the juvenile justice center?" "How did you get taken to that jail?" "I told them I was 21 years old." "Denise, you know better than to do that. Wayne and I will be there after he returns from the store."

About three hours later, Wayne and Mrs. Alice came down and brought my information with them. The guards came and got me out of the cell. I was shipped to the juvenile center until after the investigation of my case, so I was there for 2 1/2 weeks. During that time, detectives visited me and asked a few questions about what had happened. I told them I hadn't started the fight.

Three days later, the detectives found the girl I had thrown through the window, naked and dead, with a needle in her arm and shot in an alley. The girl I had cut up with the bottle was in jail for aggravated robbery of an elderly person. The judge contacted the juvenile court with a release date for me. Wayne came to visit me only once while I was there, which I was not happy about.

Finally, I appeared before the judge, who was concerned about the outcome of the matter. The judge asked, "Are you Denise Henderson?" "Yes, your honor." "Why are you in this court?" "Because I defended myself from two girls that jumped me." "You're in the court for your hearing to be released. The court finds you not guilty."

I looked over the courtroom, and saw Mrs. Alice and Wayne. I was happy because, although no one else seemed to care, my husband and his mother did. Mrs. Alice declared, "God is a way maker and he had you covered, Denise." "Yes, ma'am, and I thank Him." "You want to go to church with me Sunday?" "Sure." "Okay, we need to be there by 10:45 a.m." Mrs. Alice asked, "Wayne, don't want you to go to church with your Mama?" "No, Mama. You'll go and you'll stay in church too long." "Be careful, that's the Lord's house." It was a true joy to leave the courtroom and feel like I was going home again.

Chapter Twenty-Four

About an hour and a half later, the doctor came into the room, and looked at me with a kind expression. "Hello, Mrs. Henderson. How is it going? Any babies at home?" "No, doctor, no babies." "Well, there's going to be a baby now."

"Wayne, I'm going to take a bath and lie down for a while." "Okay, baby, I'm going to work in a few minutes." I slept all night and once again, Wayne didn't come home. I got up Sunday, went to church and had a great time with my mother-in-law. Afterward, we stopped and ate lunch before we came home and talked about the service.

The next day was a Monday, so I went to school and began looking for a job. For the next three weeks, Wayne and I spent lots of time together. As November approached, we would stay in our bedroom and never leave the house, except to go to work and school. By the middle of

November, I had begun to stay sick a lot. One day, after Wayne came home, he inquired, "Denise, are you okay? Do you need to go to the doctor?" "I think so, but not today. I'll go after school tomorrow." "Are you sure?" "Yeah, I'm fine." "Okay, I'll talk with you later." "Call me when you are on your break."

The next day I got up and went to school, but didn't stay all day. I left early and went to the Parkland Hospital emergency room, because I was feeling extremely sick, and began to bring up everything I had eaten. Checking myself in, I waited to see a doctor. An hour later, a doctor took me back into an exam room and had a nurse prepare me for some lab tests.

The nurse greeted me cheerfully. "Hello, how are you Mrs. Henderson?" "I feel a little sick, but I think I'm fine, other than that." "The doctor wants a blood and urine sample from you, so we can find out what's going on with you."

About an hour and a half later, the doctor came into the room, and looked at me with a kind expression. "Hello, Mrs. Henderson. How is it going? Any babies at home?" "No, doctor, no babies." "Well, there's going to be a baby now." I was stunned. "What? A baby?" "Yes, ma'am, you're going to have a baby. You're about four weeks pregnant." "I guess I wasn't ready for that, but I'm happy." "Good. Where's Dad? I will need for you to set up an appointment with another doctor, and will refer you to one, unless you already have a doctor." "I'll make the appointments and take the vitamins you recommended."

I left the hospital and caught the bus back home to tell Wayne about the baby. I was a little nervous, because I didn't know if Wayne was ready for children, but to be honest, it didn't matter. I was having a baby, regardless of his thoughts.

I had just made it back home when Wayne drove up at the same time. He asked, "Hey, what did the doctor say, Mrs. Henderson?" "He said we were having a baby." Wayne was surprised, as if the possibility had never occurred to him. "Are you serious?" "Yes, I'm serious. You're going to be a father, Wayne." He seemed pleased. "Man, I'm finally going to have a baby. Hell, yeah! I'm a Dad! Come on and go in the house."

As we went inside, Wayne could hardly contain himself. "Mama, guess what? We going to have a baby. What you think about that?" Mrs. Alice laughed. "A little crumb snatcher. I happy for y'all. I'm going to be a granny and I get to see my grandchildren. Yes, Lord." "The baby will have my last name." I looked at him. "You know that baby will have your name. I'm just four weeks pregnant, and I'm going to have to take it easy while I'm carrying another life inside of me."

Wayne left to tell everyone on his job and his friends. He was extremely excited and didn't know what to do with himself. Wayne walked into his job and told everyone he could find about the baby. Joe asked, "Man, you got a little one coming?" "Hell, yeah. Man, I'm happy in a mofold dude. I always wanted children."

Neither man noticed Lisa standing across room, getting extremely upset, because Wayne had been her lover for years, but didn't marry her or give her a baby. "Congratulations on your new baby, Wayne. Why wasn't I that woman for you to do these things with? I just so unhappy about all this." "Look, you already know we don't have nothing and I never wanted to marry you even when I was in the house with you. I enjoyed older women, not to marry, just to have sex with. I'm a ho sometimes, but I'm chilling on all that crap now. I have a wife and a child on the way, and all that you got going is calling my wife and talking crazy about me coming back to your house and leaving my family.

"Don't call my house no more, or there will be some problems, and I mean that. I'm going to say this only once. Don't call my house, period, or upset my wife or mother. You won't ever want to talk to me again. I'm done. Keep your ass away from me, player!"

Joe picked up the phone. "Wayne, it's Denise on the phone." "Hey, baby, can we get something to eat when you come home?" "Yes, baby, I'll be leaving in an hour." I went and lay down until Wayne came home, because I had started feeling sick again. Mrs. Alice suggested I eat a little salt. "Okay." "Let me know if you keep getting sick. I may have to take you back to the hospital." "No, I'm fine. I'm waiting to sit down with Wayne to see what he thinks about the doctor I'm scheduled to go see." "Okay, well, just let me know where to help you all." "I will."

I was having a lot of complications with the pregnancy. It didn't help that I was fighting with Wayne about him not coming home and staying out late. One night, I woke up at 2:00 a.m., and walked around to the ballroom to discover Wayne leaned up in a corner with some woman that was telling him she loved him. I listened behind him, incredulously. Finally, Wayne turned around and demanded, "What are you doing around here?" "I'm here because you wasn't home." "Go the house, I'll be home." Then he told the lady to go to her car. He got into the car with her, and left me standing there, extremely and visibly pregnant, while he began smoking a cigarette.

I could not handle this at all. While I was crying my heart out, I decided to get in touch with my older sister, Marcy White, because I had been through so much over the years. I had become isolated with people with whom I had very limited trust.

Wayne came home two days later. In the meantime, I had found Marcy, and began to visit her, sharing my experiences. One day, at Marcy's house, I told her I needed her. "I feel like I have been in this world by myself, without the support I have given to other people, but sister, I love you. Help me. I've been raped, physically beaten, abused mentally and bruised, all beginning at the age of 10 years old, with no adult to protect me, sister. I'm going to protect my child, if at all possible." My heart hurt.

Chapter Twenty-Five

The baby arrived, a little girl. who weighed six pounds and three ounces. "Oh, my, our daughter. She's beautiful, Wayne."

Two months passed, as I kept in touch with Marcy, who taught me how to take care of myself, from douching to bathing the proper way and eating with silverware. "Thank you, sister for loving me. I know you didn't know where I was, because Joyce wouldn't tell you. We have always basically been separated from each other, but everything will get better."

At around that time, Wayne asked me if I was coming home. "For what, Wayne? I'm getting tired of you disrespecting me, my mother-in-law and yourself." "Please come home. We're having a baby, Denise." "If you're unhappy, I will leave, because all this is not worth it to me anymore." "Will you let me be there when my baby is born?" "I won't stop you from being there.

Wayne, I'm not like that. I'm not going to jail because you don't respect yourself or your family. I have been dilating, so you can just meet me at the hospital in an hour." Wayne's demeanor instantly changed. "Thank you, thank you, thank you! I'll be there!"

When I got the hospital, Wayne was already there with Joe and Donnie, hanging out in the waiting room. While being prepped for delivery, I was scared to death as to what would happen next. Wayne was dressed out for delivery, and he held my hands as the contractions came. I was having an extremely hard pregnancy for the first baby, but we were both excited about the birth. Excitedly, Wayne asked me if I were doing okay. "The pain is a little strong, but I think I'll live." "Thank you for that." "For what?" "For giving me something I really wanted. A child." "No problem, Wayne. I love you." "I love you too, Denise."

I was now fully dilated, and the contractions kept coming. The doctor said, "Nurse, call in the other doctors, and let's get Mrs. Henderson into delivery." Wayne said, "Denise, we're headed to delivery. Just breathe in and out, and remember everything you learned from class. Just hold on."

As I went into the last stages of labor, the pain became so intense that I couldn't help screaming, which made Wayne nervous. Thankfully, the pain was almost over. The doctor said, "Push, Mrs. Henderson." "I'm pushing, I'm pushing!" The baby arrived, a little girl. who weighed six pounds and three ounces. "Oh, my, our daughter. She's beautiful, Wayne." "Man, she's my little angel. She's so little! Thank you, Denise, thank you so much. I wanted two kids, a boy and a girl, yes!"

He went to get his friends. "Joe, come see my daughter. Man, she's my baby forever. She have to stay at home with us, Denise, and she can't ever move out." He laughed. "Baby, you can lock her in for life," I joked. "She has to go to school and have a social life." "No, she don't. That's my seed, I'm happy as hell, bro. I don't know what to do with myself. My own daughter, she's going everywhere with me." Looking gleefully around the room, Wayne said, "That's my daughter, y'all, that's my daughter, Tanyonna Denise Henderson."

He was extremely happy about his new addition to the family, never having been a father before, and was also delighted that I was able to go home after three days. The baby had to stay in the hospital for a few more days as she was premature, but Wayne and I went to see our daughter every day until Tanyonna went home with us four days later. Wayne and I were really happy. Mrs. Alice would hold Tanyonna and laugh, saying, "Hey, granny baby!" before she began to pray over all of us.

A few days later, Mrs. Alice became curious. "So how many are y'all having?" "Wayne wants one more—a boy!" He chimed in. "I get me a boy, I'm happy with everything." Our delightful little girl kept Wayne closer to home those days.

Chapter Twenty-Six

Suddenly, two men with masks came running around the corner and saw Shelia sitting on the ground in my arms. They ran over where we were, looked at me, and then shot her in the chest.

One day, I asked Mrs. Alice if she wanted us to get an apartment, as I was going to go back to work after the baby was a year or two old, so that I could help support our family more. Wayne and I were in a good place at that time, and we stayed focused on raising our daughter, Tanyonna. As the baby was about to turn one-year old, we were preparing for her first birthday party. "Denise, what time are we going to finish getting her stuff for the party?" "Can you give me 30 minutes?" "Denise, I have to work tonight, so I'm trying to help you get everything done." "Okay, baby, here I come." "I'm putting the car seat in the car. Bring my baby out here." Alice was a little concerned. "Wayne, don't be sitting that girl in your lap while driving." "Mama, what are you talking about?" "You know, Wayne. Y'all have fun."

We left the house and headed to the Town East mall to finish picking up the party items. Just when we put the baby in her stroller and walked into the store, we heard shooting, but we weren't sure where it was coming from. "Wayne, where is that noise coming from?" "Those are gunshots, Denise. Let's get out of here." As soon as we turned around, I heard someone call, "Denise! Help me!" As she was running across the parking lot I realized that I knew the young lady. It was Shelia.

I said, "Wayne, get my baby." "Where are you going?" "That's my friend. Please, I need to help her. Take my baby and go." "You don't know what that lady is into. I'm not going to let you get into that, Denise." There wasn't time to argue. "Please Wayne, just get my daughter and go, get her out of harm's way. Shelia already called me by name. Please go."

Shelia ran up to me, and I saw she was crying. She said, "I'm sorry for everything I did to you." "Just be quiet, Shelia." "No, Denise, I set you up to be murdered, because Brian used to rape me when I was little, but I fell in love with him. You came and took him away from me. I told his two daughters you sent him to jail and had him murdered in prison." I saw that she was hurt. "Shelia, you're bleeding." She had been shot in the back.

I asked someone to call an ambulance. "I forgive you, Shelia. Just stop talking." "There's still a hit out on you. Please forgive me, Denise. You're a good person. I'm sorry. Be careful. I tried to stop it, but I can't, and I don't know who's coming after you now." "Don't worry about it."

Suddenly, two men with masks came running around the corner and saw Shelia sitting on the ground in my arms. They ran over where we were, looked at me, and then shot her in the chest. I screamed and cried. One of the men said, "Nasty bitch, you won't give anyone else AIDS or take their money." "Shelia, I don't understand. God." But she was already gone, dying in my arms.

Wayne came back for me a minute later and told me to stop crying. "Baby, where is Tanyonna?" "She's with your sister and Joe. Are you okay?" "I'm not injured, but Shelia was shot in the back before she reached me. Then two men with masks shot her again while she was in my arms, and they said she would never give anyone else AIDS or take their money. Shelia said that they had put out a hit on me." "Why did she put the hit out, and what did she say?" "Shelia said it was because I had taken Brian from her, and that he always treated me differently from the other girls and women. Shelia told Brian's two daughters I had him locked up and murdered. That was the biggest lie ever told by anyone about me. That's crazy, Wayne." "So, do we know who the person is who is acting on the hit?" "No, honestly, I didn't even know all this was going on, Wayne, but I know who's involved and that helps. I have to wait a minute to talk to the police." "I know, Denise." "Wayne, please check on the baby." "Okay, I will."

The police asked me questions about what Shelia had told me, and about my past experiences with her. The officers gave me their business cards. "We'll be in contact. Thank you for your help, ma'am." Wayne asked, "Are y'all done asking questions to my wife?" He turned to me. "Can we let Marcy keep my daughter until we finish shopping? Baby, I don't want her in the stores right now." "That's fine. I feel the same way." "Okay, I'm going to run you to the house to change clothes, since there's blood all over you."

"Yeah, that would be good. I could take a shower and then we can leave. Thank you, Wayne." "For what?" "For being here." "Denise, you're my wife and although I don't do everything right, I love you. And you're the only woman I ever loved like this." I gave him a kiss and a hug. "Let's go and get this little baby girl."

We talked with Marcy and Joe for a few minutes, and Marcy agreed to take Tanyonna with her until we were finished shopping for her birthday party. Joe went back to work. "Thanks, man, for coming to help." Joe said, "That's what friends do, man. We'll talk later."

I finished getting dressed, and we sat and talked about the incident. Wayne tried to reassure me. "Everything is going to be okay." "I'm fine, Wayne. Things happen for a reason, the elderly say." "Let's go, Denise." "Yeah, I guess we'll try going out to the store again. Everything will work out."

We went out shopping for the second time that day to finish purchasing birthday items for our daughter, as she was turning a year old in two days. We got everything done in four hours, and headed back to the house to drop some things off. We picked up Tanyonna and talked with Marcy for a little while. "Denise, things have sure been crazy today!" "Yes, but I'm learning about people and how they think. I didn't realize what was going on around me, sis." "Denise, you were young then, and still have even more to learn now, honey." I decided to explain the entire story to her, and how I knew Shelia.

"I knew Erica from the school I was attending at the time, and I even stayed with her and her strange family when me and Mama was having issues, if that's what you want to call it. However, Erica and I could no longer stay at her house. Honestly, I witnessed her father having sex with her. Her biological father! But I never said anything, because I was hoping she would talk to me, so I never said anything. Her mom knew also, but when Erica and I stayed at Shelia's house, it was crazy there, too, with the stepdad I found out two weeks ago was already sleeping with Shelia from when she was ten years old until she was 16. Her mother would have sex with them or watch."

Marcy said, "That's ridiculous." "Honestly, I didn't realize, sis. I have been raped since I was a child, and when I met Brian, he raped me so much when I was a kid, and then he started giving me things—really nice things. I became accustomed to it, and thought that's the way life's supposed to be, that's not being taught." "What do you mean?" "I fell in love with a man who stole love from me and didn't earn it. I was child, Marcy. Brian treated me mostly good, except when he jumped on me for being at a club dancing with another guy. What was crazy, though, was that he was raping me basically every night that I stayed with him. He also raped Erica and his stepdaughter, Shelia, for years. Erica fell in love with Brian, too, but when he became tired of things, she came up missing."

"Where was our Mom during all of this?" "Joyce was not wanting me to stay with her, and most of the time I couldn't find her. When she moved, I spent a year looking for her while I was going through this. And I couldn't find you, because you were on the trucks and no one cared to tell me anything." "What about Sherry? Where was she?" "In south Dallas, and I left because the husband of the lady who had raised her got naked one night as I slept in the living room, and lay on top of me. When I woke up, he put his hand over my mouth and I bit his finger. I began talking loudly, telling him to leave me alone. His wife and Sherry came in and found us, and he tried to lie his way out, but he was naked and I had all my clothes on. Of course, my sister Sherry asked me to leave their house, because she had been secretly sleeping with that man. I'm just glad that I'm learning so much right now, sis." "I'm sorry all of this is going on, but you're a strong person and you're going to do well for yourself. Just keep going, Denise. Keep going."

Wayne commented that having my sister around was good for me. Marcy agreed. "I love you, Denise. This road may get a little harder but keep going." "I have to get ready to go sis, but I love you too. And thank you for keeping Tanyonna. And you be encouraged, I think I take a lot of things from my big sister." I laughed at my last remark. "Yes Denise, I'm sure. You guys enjoy your day and I never mind watching my niece." "I'll see you later. Take care."

Wayne asked me, "Are you ready to go home, or do you need to eat now?" "I'm definitely hungry." "Where would you like to go?" "Let's go to the Pancake House and get some pancakes.

Hey, Mama's baby makes her look so pretty. I love having a daughter, Wayne. Thank you, baby daddy," and laughed at my own joke. "No, I'm her father. My daughter wears my name, and I'm married to her mother. That's the difference, baby." "I got it." We left for the Pancake House.

After lunch, we went home and continued to prepare for our daughter's party. A few days later, the party was packed with children at a Chuck E. Cheese, and Tanyonna was afraid of the purple ape. The turnout was great. Tanyonna got a lot of gifts and toys, and everything was awesome.

Wayne stood up and made a little speech. "I thank everyone for coming out, and thanks for everything." I laughed and exclaimed, "Well, our summer baby is a mess. She's making a mess everywhere."

Chapter Twenty-Seven

I was going to church some, but still didn't have the full concept of God and the operation of the Lord. When Wayne came back home, I didn't even make a fuss, not this time.

Four months later, as we were getting ready to go to the car dealership to get a second car, I realized that I was feeling awful. "Baby, what's wrong?" Wayne asked. "I'm just feeling sick and everything smells bad to me. Maybe I need some crackers or something." "You might be pregnant again." "I don't think so, Wayne." "Well, I don't know. You need to see a doctor." Mrs. Alice said, "Girl, you're pregnant again. I'm going to move out on you all." She laughed. I don't know if I'm pregnant or not, but I'll make a doctor's appointment soon." Wayne said, "Go ahead and call tomorrow, and I will take off work." "Okay, I'll call for an appointment."

A few days later, I went to see my obstetrician for a pregnancy test. "How are you today, Denise?" "Well, I haven't been feeling well, so Wayne and I thought I should come in and see if another baby is on the way." "The nurse will be here shortly. Mrs. Henderson, are you looking for another child?" Wayne answered for me. "Yes, if she's pregnant, what can I say?" "I remember you stating that you wanted two, a boy and a girl." "That's right, doctor."

The nurse arrived about that time, and I was instructed to go the bathroom and urinate in a cup, and when I returned, the nurse drew some blood. The doctor and nurse left, and were gone for what seemed like a long time. I began wondering why they were taking so long to come back. Wayne said, "Just wait. It ain't like they don't know we're here." "Very funny, Wayne."

The nurse then entered into room. "Denise, the results are back and the doctor will come see you in a moment. Okay?" When the doctor returned he asked again, "How are you feeling now?" "I'm fine." "Well, I think we need to say that you're going to be a mother again. Stay on your task with an eye on your future, because you're going to be a busy young lady, Mrs. Henderson." He laughed, then continued. "Now please, make an appointment to follow up with me throughout the pregnancy, if possible, and thanks for coming in today. I'll see you next time." We thanked the doctor.

As we headed home, we made plans for another child. Wayne said, "I have to work some additional hours to make sure we are prepared for the baby." "No, I can go ahead and work until I'm nine months, Wayne. I'll be fine." "No, just wait until the kids are a certain age and then we can talk about that. Just go to school. Mama will help us when she can, and so will a few other family members." "Are you sure, Wayne? Because I know we need the money right now." "It's okay. Let's just plan to go this route right now and see how everything will work." "All right."

After we got home, Wayne helped me get Tanyonna ready for bed and then left, saying he'd be back shortly. "Where are you going, Wayne?" "The fish place." "Okay, see you later."

I woke up the next morning and found Wayne asleep on the couch. I woke him up, and asked him what time he came home. He said about 4:30 a.m., because he got on the clock to help the owner transport cases of fish to other stores. "Well, I wish you would have called me and let me know what was going on." "Baby, you were asleep and I didn't want to wake you and Tanyonna." "So, when do you have to be back at work?" "I have to be back at 9:00 in the morning. Denise, the owner is going to Houston this weekend for a convention to cater, and he needs 50 employees to attend. I told him I would be available, because we need the money." "Wayne, you didn't have a chance to talk to me about it?" "No, I had to answer immediately if I wanted to go, because he was making reservations while we were at work." "I understand. Are you going to be gone the whole weekend?" "Yes, and I'll be back Monday. I'm leaving tomorrow." "I'll help you pack your things." "Baby, that's nice of you to take care of me like that." "Why not? You take care of me and your daughter."

I had no idea that Wayne was also meeting Lisa there and would be spending time with her the whole weekend. She still wanted him to choose her instead of me.

The next morning, I dropped off Wayne to meet his boss, as they prepared to leave for Houston. Wayne asked, "You have the money I gave you to feed everyone?" "Yes." "Thank you for packing my things. I love you too, and I will call when available. Okay?" "No problem. See you later."

Wayne and the other employees left, some in the company van and some in their own cars. Wayne drove the van, and was excited about leaving home to meet Lisa. It took them 3 1/2 hours to get to Houston, and additional time to get set up in their rooms. After Wayne made it to his room, he called Lisa to join him. Although their relationship had been broken off for a while after Wayne had sex with another young lady who had lived with Lisa, Wayne and Lisa had been dating each other again for several months.

Wayne would work with the owner in the daytime, then would hurry back to his room and meet Lisa every night to sleep with her. Lisa managed to get Wayne back with her when they got back to Dallas. "Wayne, I really miss you." "Yeah? How much?" "More than you know. Please come home. I will do whatever you want."

"Man, I have to take care of my kids and Denise is pregnant again." Her eyes widened. "Wow, I didn't know that. So, what are you going to do?" "Nothing. I'm having my child, if you're implying I should get rid of it." "No, I'm just wondering." "And I'm not dealing with no women can't help me take care of my children. She don't want them around. She damn sure don't want me." "I love you, Wayne. I will help do what you want. Just come back and stay with me." "All right, but I'm not taking my clothing from the house." "You don't need to. I'll buy you some clothes." "Cool!"

After Wayne returned to Dallas on Monday, he made things seem as if there were no problems between us, but two days later, he became upset because I asked him to take the trash out. "Wayne, the garbage has overflowed in the kitchen. Can you take it out to the dumpster please?" "Why the hell everyone waits until I get home to take out the trash?" "Because I take care of your daughter and mother, Wayne, and I'm getting ready to go to church with your mother."

Wayne received a call from Lisa on Alice's phone. He answered and pretended that Lisa was calling from work, and said he was on the way to work on a Friday night. "Denise, I have to go to work. I'll see you later. Have a good time at church." Wayne kissed Tanyonna and me, and left for 2 1/2 weeks.

I was going to church some, but still didn't have the full concept of God and the operation of the Lord. When Wayne came back home, I didn't even make a fuss, not this time. I began to start preparing to have my next baby by living on my own. I filed for Section 8 housing, food stamps, WIC and other state-sponsored help that was available. At eight months of my pregnancy, Wayne showed up at Mrs. Alice's house, where I was living with Tanyonna. His woman, Lisa, was in the car waiting for him. Wayne took too long to come out, so Lisa knocked on the door and asked to speak to him. I answered the door and when I saw who it was, I said, "Wayne, come to the door." "What is it, Denise?" "Apparently your other woman wants you." "What the hell are you talking about?" "Wayne, stop playing games and come to the door." "I'll be back." He left, cussing, and didn't come back for another week and a half.

At this point, I was tired of it and decided it was time to do something about it. "Mrs. Alice, me and my babies are going to move out soon. I am tired of Wayne mistreating me and I signed up for housing. I can move in soon after finding a place I like." "Baby, don't be in a hurry. Wayne is acting silly right now." "I understand why you say that, Mrs. Alice, because you want us to stay together and raise our children. But I can't do this anymore! I love you for always being here for us, but it's just time for me to move on with my life. He jumps on me, cheats on me and it's getting where he don't want to do anything for us at times. Maybe because of Lisa, I really don't know anymore, but I have to prepare to do what's best for me and my children. If it means leaving to do better, then that's what it's going to be from here on out."

Mrs. Alice said, "I will never encourage you to leave your husband, no matter what I or anyone else may think. That has to be your decision. Denise, I love you like you're my daughter and you have a good heart, honey. Never allow anyone to steal that from you." "Of course not, Mrs. Alice. I have to believe everything is going to get better whichever way things are led to move." "Please let me know anything I can do to help you or the children." "I will."

A few weeks later, I was standing outside, talking to my sister Sherry, when my water broke. People ran into the house to call the ambulance, which arrived about ten minutes later. The paramedic asked me how I was. "I'm okay right now." "Has your water broken?" "Yes." "Are you feeling contractions, such as a push on your ovaries?" "Not at the moment." "We're going to take your vital signs and transport you to Parkland Hospital. Is that okay?" "Yes, thank you."

After he checked my vital signs, he asked, "Is anyone coming with you?" "Yes, my sister Lenise. That's her standing to the left of you in a white shirt, jeans and her hair in a ponytail. She's waving at us." He turned to Lenise. "Okay, we're ready to take Mrs. Henderson to the hospital." "Thanks, I'm coming with you."

I asked Sherry, "Would you please take Tanyonna to stay with Mrs. Alice? I'll call her as soon as we get to the hospital." Lenise said, "Just bring her with us, and they can come get her from the hospital." "Okay, just put here in here with me."

We made it to Parkland in 15 minutes. Immediately, the doctor and nurse took me back for prepping. Thirty minutes later, Mrs. Alice showed up with Wayne. The doctors asked him questions, and later, Wayne was dressed and going into the delivery room with me. "How are you doing, Denise?" "I'm fine. How are you?" "Good. Let's have this baby and it's going to be a boy, too." "Well, I will be happy with either one, a boy or a girl."

After about an hour, the contractions started coming, and I was ready to get it over with. I had a boy who was six pounds and five ounces, just as handsome as can be, and we named him Daquan Wayne Henderson. The doctor said, "You all have a beautiful baby boy. We're going to put him on oxygen for a little while until his breathing catches up with him. Wayne asked, "What's wrong with him, Doc?" "Minor issue with his breathing, but he's going to be just fine because his lungs are very strong." I said I wanted to hold him. "No problem, Mrs. Henderson."

I stayed in the hospital for three days, then went home with Daquan. Wayne was home for a week with me and our children, and also spent time at work.

Chapter Twenty-Eight

He saw a hammer, picked it up and hit me in the head with it twice. Blood splattered everywhere, while Tanyonna ran out of the room and watched her mother being beaten almost unconscious.

About ten months later, Wayne had been staying out off and on with Lisa. Finally, one day, while Wayne was at work, I had fed the children and had put them down for a nap, when there was a knock on the door. It was Lisa. "How can I help you?" "I need to talk to you. I want to know; can you leave my man alone?" "What?" "I'm talking about Wayne!" "What about Wayne?" "I'm in love with him, and we're trying to have our own family. I've been fucking him for 3 1/2 years, and he lives with me now. He don't want you. He want a real woman like me who can make him feel right every night and take care of him. I can do that for his ass and bitch, I want you to leave my man alone, because he told me he is getting ready to divorce you."

I said, "First of all, I've had enough of your reduced intellect. Second, Wayne is a married man, and consider yourself with a deficiency if you're listening to all those lies he is feeding you now, and all the ones you believed in for the last three or four years. And lastly, I don't particularly give a damn about what you and Wayne have going on, but if you don't get your commercial-looking ass away from this door, you will despise the day you ever laid eyes on me. Now, you have less than a split second to move away from our door, or trust me I will remove you. Oh, and have a nice day." I waited for Lisa's response. All she said was, "Bitch!" as she walked away, never to return again.

Four days later, Wayne showed up at the house one afternoon, saying nothing. I could tell that something was wrong with him. I assumed that Lisa and he had words, and that it didn't go well. He went to the bedroom and got on the phone to Lisa, and I could hear him begging Lisa to stop being upset with him. I wasn't overly sure how I should have handled all this, but after a little while, although I became upset, I didn't want confusion around our children.

All of a sudden, Wayne exploded out of the bedroom to the living room, while I was talking to Mrs. Alice about going to church that night. He was cussing at us both. "Nobody asked you to start shit." Then he hauled off and slapped me, dragged me through the living room to the kitchen and back to the hallway. I tried to get loose from him and grabbed anything I could. I got a knife and tried to get him off me while Mrs. Alice screamed, "Leave her alone and get out of the house." "Shut the hell up, ain't nobody talking to you."

He saw a hammer, picked it up and hit me in the head with it twice. Blood splattered everywhere, while Tanyonna ran out of the room and watched her mother being beaten almost unconscious. I was crying and both babies were crying, and Tanyonna was telling her Daddy to stop hitting her Mommy. Tanyonna tried to pull Wayne off me, and then William came into the room. He saw blood everywhere, and his mother was still yelling at Wayne to get out.

By this time, my right eye was black and swollen. William fought him and said, "You don't put your hand on no female, fool. Fight me, I'm a man." Mrs. Alice called the police and the ambulance, and they immediately rushed me to the hospital to make sure that I stayed alive. I lost almost 700 cc of blood from the openings in my head, and blood was also coming from the side of my right eye. My head was stitched up in two places and for the rest of my life, hair would not grow in those areas. I had to stay out of school for a while, because I couldn't see clearly with all the head trauma, and my right eye developed some vision issues.

The police arrived, questioned Wayne, immediately handcuffed him and took him to the Lew Sterrett Justice Center on Commerce Street. He was charged with domestic violence and attempted murder, in addition to some outstanding warrants and tickets. The domestic violence charges alone kept him in jail for several weeks. Lisa went to the jail to visit him any time he could have visitors, and put money on his books so he could buy extra food. "Baby, don't worry. I'm going to get you out of here." "What the lawyer say, Lisa?" "He's coming to see you tomorrow, and if Denise will drop the charges, you'll have to pay a fine. But it won't be jail time unless you don't comply with the courts." "Okay." "Baby, I got you. I hope you'll marry me, Wayne. I was supposed to have been your wife anyway." "We'll talk about it, baby. I got a lot on me right now. Just be here to help your man, baby. I'm not going nowhere, so stop tripping." "I know. I love you, Wayne." "I love you, too. Chill, baby."

Wayne stayed in jail for almost a month, and finally was released because Lisa called downtown, pretending to be me, and asked them to drop the charges. However, the District Attorney's office wanted to know why I would do that, so they sent me a letter and requested that I show up at their office with identification on a scheduled date. By this time, my Section 8 housing application had come through, and I had moved to a two-bedroom place in Oak Cliff with Tonyanna and Dajuan. I didn't get the letter, because Mrs. Alice didn't know how to contact me, so the letter sat at Mrs. Alice's house unopened.

A month went by, and the DA had no contact number for me, except Alice's house. The case was reduced to domestic violence, and since Wayne had never been to jail before for anything except traffic tickets, and had never been convicted of a felony, they only required Wayne to attend anger management classes and do community service. He also had 40 hours of substance abuse class to attend.

As soon as he completed these legal requirements, he went back to being with Lisa. Around 2 1/2 months after he moved in with Lisa, the owner of the fish place fired him. Wayne met a guy who started selling drugs in the apartments in central Oak Cliff. He had been tied up with this guy for months after getting out of jail and losing his job. However, I had state help with the kids, and I got a part-time job to help keep the kids and me above water.

Wayne had gotten to where he wouldn't help me, and I eventually stopped asking him for help. I moved on, and tried to make it without worrying family and friends. But one day, my welfare check was going to be late, so I contacted my mother and asked to borrow $15 for Pampers until my check came. Joyce asked, "Where is they daddy, because I have to pay my bills, and I have something else to do. I can't help you, sorry. I'll talk to you later." I hung up the phone and cried.

I learned how to put towels on the baby and pin both sides closed, and then wash them out like a diaper. I did that all weekend until my check came that Monday. Joyce called, and made time to talk. "Hey, Mama baby. What are you doing today?" "Getting my kids ready so I can go and get the things they need. Pampers, clothing and food." "Oh, okay. I was trying to catch you and see if you can help me with my electric bill." "How much is it?" "Two hundred, but I only need $125 so they won't turn it off tomorrow." "Mama, I have it, but I want to be able to get my kids things they need." "Well, I guess we just have to be here in the dark. I'll try to get help from the payment places this week and I hope they have money left, because Anthony is here and have to eat." Her guilt trip on me worked. "Okay, Mama, I will pay it for you." "I appreciate it. Can you bring it over here?" "I don't have a way over there." "Didn't you say someone is taking you somewhere?" "Yes, Mama, but I'm paying them to go to the store." "Well, don't you know how to give them a few more dollars to bring you over here? The more try I try to teach, you the dumber you get. Girl, bring that money over here. I got to go. Call me and let me know when you're on the way."

Honestly, I didn't have extra money, but I wanted to help Joyce keep her lights on. "My kids need their things. I'm just not going to buy myself nothing. It's okay, I'll be okay." Two hours later, I was at the second store, buying my children Pampers, milk and other items. When I finished, I called Joyce from a pay phone. She was upset because it was taking me hours to get her the $125 that I really didn't have. "Mama, I'm on my way over there." "Why in the hell is it taking you so long?" "I have to get my kids some things." "You need to come on with your slow ass."

Joyce had her friends over at her house, putting me down, speaking about how worthless I was, and that that was why her husband got another woman that got it going on. "Hell, I have always said Denise ain't going to be shit. Like her daddy, he ain't shit either." Her neighbor, Mrs. Ross, spoke up. "Denise seems like a fine child, respectful, and she don't have a problem helping you, even though you should have paid your own bills, instead of helping people who honestly can help themselves or may not even appreciate you doing it, Joyce." "I ain't worried about all that." "Mama, here is the money. Don't worry about paying me back, I'm going to be okay." "All right

You sure you don't need it back?" "I'm okay. I have to go, Mama."

I kissed her on the cheek and left. I felt sad for a moment, but I never had the idea that I was powerful in spirit. I wasn't totally in that known place in Christ, but I was covered. I headed back home with my babies, crying because they were hungry and wet. The people who had taken me to the store were owed $25 for taking me to the different places. When the driver helped me get the children and shopping out of the car, I thanked him and tried to give him the money. But the driver said, "Blessed is the man that walk in the Lord. You keep the money, Denise and buy something that makes you happy." "No, I don't mind paying you." "Okay, you are a nice person with a wonderful heart. Just make me happy and stay that way, okay? I love you, young lady. Take care of them babies."

Chapter Twenty-Nine

Furious, Wayne pulled a handgun on me, slapped me and said, "I'll kill you, Denise." He pointed the gun at me and dared me to walk out of the bedroom. The gun was pointed straight at my forehead.

Two months later, I received a call from Wayne. "Hello, Denise, how are you?" "I'm all right, considering the challenges at times, but I'm fine. How can I help you, Wayne?" "I miss you and I want to see my children." "Wayne, I've never tried to stop you from seeing your babies. But all the fighting for no apparent reason makes no sense." "Please let me visit my kids. What do I have to do? I'll do whatever you want. I'm sorry for hurting you baby, but it was the alcohol and my casual drug use, but I'm better. I've been to anger management and doing everything I'm supposed to. Please, Denise." I hesitated. "I can bring them next week to visit, okay?" "Baby I have to wait that long?" "Yes Wayne, they're resting right now." "All right. When are you coming?" "I'll come over to your mother's and bring them." "That's cool. Come on Saturday." "Saturday? Why?" "The kids don't have to be anywhere Sunday, maybe church if you're taking them." "I'll be there at your mother's house by 6:00 p.m."

The next Saturday, I was concerned about going over to Mrs. Alice's house, mostly because of the negative experiences, but basically, because I didn't know what to expect from Wayne this time. He didn't like the fact that I had moved the children out of the house, because I'd never gotten over him attacking me. Out of all the wrong Wayne was doing, I never found out what had actually happened in his domestic violence court case. I didn't know that Lisa had lied about the charges being dropped, and didn't know about the mail sitting in Mrs. Alice's bedroom.

I took Tanyonna and Dajuan to Mrs. Alice's house at 6:00 p.m., just as I had promised. Wayne appeared to be fine at the beginning of the visit. We sat around and talked, and the children played with their granny. Then Wayne suggested that we go out and get the kids something to eat. "Where are we going?" "Wherever you want to, but you know that they'll eat McDonald's." I smiled. "Yes, they will." "Let's go. I just want to talk to you beforehand, as I have something to do." Okay."

We got in his car, and as we were driving to McDonald's, Wayne began talking. "Denise, are you going to come back to me? I miss you and my kids." "I know you miss them, and we can work on how we will deal with our children." "What do you mean?" "I'm just saying give yourself time to do what you want to do to get better, honey. That's all." "I'm already better, Denise," he insisted. "Then show me. You hurt me, Wayne, and I never did anything to you up to that point." "Denise, spend the night with me." "No, I plan to go home." "Can I go home with you?" "No, we need to work on all of this, Wayne." Wayne appeared upset. As we returned to his mother's house, he hugged me and said, "I love you." Then he left.

I never thought that something would happen so quickly afterwards. I was still at Mrs. Alice's house, sitting with her and the children, when Wayne returned about 40 minutes later, acting strangely. He played with the kids for a few minutes, then asked me to come to the bedroom to talk. "Wayne, what is this about?" "Please, just come and talk to me." Mrs. Alice said, "Wayne, don't you be starting nothing in my house. I have told you." "Mama, I just want to talk to Denise about my children." "Don't touch that girl. I'm not playing with you." "Mama, I'm all right." We went into the back room and talked for about an hour. Then, all of a sudden, Wayne lost his cool.

"Denise, you're not going to leave me." I asked him what he was talking about. "I just want to be happy, Wayne. I'm 18 years old, stressing over things don't matter." "You're not leaving." "I'm getting the kids and going home."

Furious, Wayne pulled a handgun on me, slapped me, and said, "I'll kill you, Denise." He pointed the gun at me and dared me to walk out of the bedroom. The gun was pointed straight at my forehead. "Put that gun down. Haven't you hurt me enough, Wayne?" "Denise, I never meant to hurt you. I'm sorry, but you can't leave and live." "I'm tired of all this." Wayne fired the gun, and the bullet went through the wall to an empty apartment. I cried and screamed at him, "You need help. I want my kids!" "You're not leaving out of this room."

Then I heard Mrs. Alice say, "If you don't open that door I'm kicking it in and calling the police. Let that girl out of there now!" "I let her out the minute you go sit down." Mrs. Alice kicked the door in. Wayne was shaking me while I lay on the end of the bed, crying. I said, "Mrs. Alice, watch my babies. Protect them, please." I didn't know that the lady next door already had my kids at her house, and that Mrs. Alice had called the police.

Wayne had his hand around my neck, with a .45 handgun pointed at my face. He was so high and drunk he was sweating really badly. Wayne had no idea that his mother had also called William to come over. He got the gun out of Wayne's hand before the police arrived.

I got off the bed and went to the bathroom to wipe my face. Mrs. Alice asked me, "Are you okay, honey?" "Yes, I'm okay. Where are my babies?" "They're next door." "I want to see my children and take them home. Mrs. Alice, I'm done with your son. I'm leaving and I will never return to be with him. I promise that if I plan a serious relationship in the future, you will always be in your grandchildren's lives. That's a promise. And thank you for loving me all these years. But I need to move on."

Mrs. Alice began to cry. "I'm sorry for all you've been through, and I want you to know that as long as I live, you are always welcome wherever I am." I began to cry. "Thank you, you have always been a great mother figure and positive person in my life, and I will never forget you, ever. Besides, your grandchildren love you to death. Goodbye, Mrs. Alice, we'll see you around."

As for Wayne, he was taken to jail for causing a disturbance. The police never knew that Wayne had a gun, or that he had drawn it around me or anyone else. He was in jail for two days, before being released, as Lisa bailed him out. They continued to live together. A year after all of this, I heard that Wayne had gotten caught up with a guy from Shy-town (Chicago) and the guy had built a drug house in the apartments Mrs. Alice lived in. Before long, almost everyone in the apartments was smoking cocaine. Other drug houses opened in the back units, and even the children were smoking. Some elderly people and some 12-year-olds were strung out so badly that they were prostituting on the corner in front of the complex, so that they could get money for their drugs. One morning, information was shared with me that the FBI and the Texas Rangers were looking for the head guy, Wayne and some other people. The task force raided the entire complex because an undercover agent bought three kilos of cocaine from four separate dealers in the same complex. Two days later, Wayne was arrested for murder and drug distribution and trafficking. He was convicted and sentenced to 20 years in the state prison. He had never been convicted of a felony before in his life.

Chapter Thirty

"Denise, don't do that." "Don't do what? You wanted this, and I've been through so much in my life. Men like you come often, and I don't know what I'm going to do, but I know me and my son will make it somehow."

Afterwards, the city and state shut down the Oak Cliff apartments and condemned them. Mrs. Alice had to find somewhere else to live, and she had to fight to keep her Section 8 housing, because Wayne had lived in the apartment with her. As for me, I was getting myself together, but was still married to Wayne. Someone introduced me to a guy named Keith Halston. We dated for two years. One day, he asked me, "How are you, Denise?" "Great, Keith. I'm pregnant." The baby would be a boy. Keith was happy about it. Then he said, "I guess I can't retire from the school soon, because I have another child to take care of, but I will be there when it's born. I promise I will, and throughout the duration." "Keith, I have been through so much in my life, and I'm not willing to give my life to someone who really don't want to be introduced to that side of me."

One day, just before I was due to give birth, I was sitting at home wondering if Keith had a wife at home. "Keith, would you take me to your house?" He complied, without any issues or complaints. "Denise, you are an amazing person and I never want you to stop being an awesome woman." "Thank you, Keith. You are a great person. All I ask is that you support your son, no matter what happens with us. Although I would love to raise your son, Keith Miles Harrison, with you, I would appreciate at least that much." "Let's be positive and take one day at a time." I'm okay with that. And thank you for allowing me to visit your home. I love it, by the way. It's just beautiful." "No problem. Denise, I do want to share that I am separated from my girlfriend. Alex

Dawn is her name, and we have dated over 2 1/2 years. Listen, I was really glad when my sister Tonya introduced us to one another. Honestly, I wasn't sure what we would do as far as a relationship, but you are so cute and totally fine."

I laughed. "You're something else Keith, but thank you. Did you think we would be having a baby?" "Yes, because after a year of dating you, I asked you for a baby, didn't I?" "Yes, you did, Keith. However, I didn't think you was serious, until you allowed me to take your car and pick you up from the elementary school where you worked nights, giving me funding, helping me pay a few bills at my house when you had your own house, and when I was pregnant, to assure we wasn't hungry or anything else. And most of all, thank you for overall being here this far."

After appreciating each other, we went to dinner and a movie afterwards. Keith took me home to get some rest. About 7:00 p.m. the next evening, I was home with my kids when my water broke. I called the ambulance and my sister Sherry to come and see about Tanyonna and Dajuan. My neighbor came over later to find out if my baby was coming. However, I contacted Keith's sister Tonya, and she called him at work to give him the address of the hospital. He arrived and smiled. "Hello, Denise, how are you doing?"

The doctor came into the room and shared with was going on with me. He asked Keith if he would be there for the delivery of his child. "Sure, that's why I'm here." "Okay, the nurse will be in shortly to bring you what you need to dress out." "No problem. I'm definitely ready to see my child born." The doctor laughed.
"First one?" "Yes, by Denise."

Finally, Keith was ready and entered the room where I was waiting to deliver. As I went into the last stages of labor, the pain became extremely intense, and I was screaming. "Keith,

I'm sorry, but it's just so painful." "Denise, push and breathe in and out, just relax. This will all be over soon. Hold on, Denise, you can do it." "It hurts so bad!"

Finally, the baby boy appeared, 7 pounds and 14 ounces. Both of us were smiling, because Keith had wanted a boy. We named him Keith Miles Halston and were so happy. While I was still in the hospital, Keith visited daily before going to work as a custodian supervisor at a Dallas elementary school. He was a man who liked having nice things, and at the time had taken care of all his children. He had quite a few women who had mothered his kids. Things was going great— at least, for him. Keith took his son and me home when we were discharged, and made sure the baby had milk, Pampers and clothing so that I would be okay until the child needed more. Keith was a great father for a while, and we called him Big Keith. After his son turned two, however, he began acting strangely. One day, I called him to come by and bring some Pampers. "Hi, Keith, how are you?" "I'm good. Running some errands. What's going on with you?" "I want to know when you are able to come by the house, because little Keith needs some Pampers. I've tried to call you since this morning, and there was no answer." "Denise, I may have been asleep and didn't hear the phone." "Okay, that's fine. Can you come by today to either bring money or the Pampers?" "You don't have any money on you right now?" "If I had money, I would have already bought my son some Pampers." Keith was quiet for a moment. "Okay, I will get by before I go to work." I was annoyed. "All right. Goodbye!" "What's wrong with you?" "Nothing. I'm fine." "Are you upset about something?" "Keith, it really doesn't matter if I'm upset with you when it comes to me personally, but don't mistreat my baby. You asked for a child, Keith, and you can't seem to find it enough for you. You have a child living next door, and your family has been sharing with me about the other children you have. My thing is to take care of your baby." "Denise, I do take care of my son. What are you talking about?" "I'm not going down that road. If you don't know, then it doesn't become my job to remind you of your responsibilities. I won't be doing that. However, I will never stop you from seeing little Keith, but what I'm not doing is playing games with you because you think being stupid is cute." "Denise, we need to talk. I'll be by there in an hour. Don't act like that. I do what I'm suppose to." "I don't want to hear your game playing. I've been through too much." "Okay, I'll see you shortly."

He showed up 1 1/2 hours later with five boxes of Pampers, a case and a half of formula, and some small jumpers for little Keith. Big Keith looked stressed. "You all right, Denise?" "I'm fine." "Can we talk?" Sure." "I want you to know I love you. Do you remember when I told you me and my girlfriend was separated?" "Yes, I remember." "Well, we're considering getting back together, but not fully yet. Meaning we're not living together. I'm in love with her and I love her, and I'm sorry, Denise."

"So, let me get this straight. You came into my life to add drama and make things more complicated than what I have already been through, by being with me five years. Now you tell me that you and this chick you have been separated from all these years have decided to get back together. Maybe my question is, were you talking while and since we had little Keith?" "Yes, but not seeing each other, because she was with someone else, because I was cheating on her." "And that's cute. Keith, do you know how dangerous that is? So, you're wanting me to take our son and move on with my life. What kind of man are you? Never, mind, don't answer that." "Denise, don't do that." "Don't do what? You wanted this, and I've been through so much in my life. Men like you come often, and I don't know what I'm going to do, but I know me and my son will make it somehow." "To answer your question regarding what I want you do, move on when time allows you to. I don't want that, but I know you're not going to wait on me to see if me and my girlfriend make it." "Hell, no. That's not going to happen. All I ask is that you take care of your baby, Keith." He insisted that he loved his son. "Of course, I'm going to take care of him. I have to go to work Denise." "Okay, well, see you whenever." "I'm going to take care of my son because I love him."

Chapter Thirty-One

The next night, I asked my sister Barbra to baby-sit while I went out on a date with Darren. He drove up in a Cadillac and got out of the door with some beautiful flowers, knocked on the door and gave me a kiss.

Days, months and before I knew it, years had passed. Keith stopped checking on little Keith, and he even stopped calling. He changed jobs and moved. Three years after I last saw him, Keith married the girlfriend he was separated from, and right before the marriage, Keith had a little girl by another woman and left her with the baby.

After Keith married, he had two kids by his wife, and left all the other children fatherless. He lied to his wife and said that none of the children were his, but he was at the hospitals with some of them and was taking care of them. Little Keith was abandoned by his father, and struggled later in life as he grew up.

I began to get a little closer to my family so that I would have some sort of support. Of course, Barbra and Marcy had always been available when I needed to talk to someone. One day, I met with two of my sisters and one of my brothers (my oldest brother, Jason Miller). We went to the Pancake House in Dallas and talked about my baby's father, Keith.

I said, "Thank you guys for coming. It's been 1 1/2 years since I last saw Keith, and I was so angry at how he did little Keith and not visiting, taking care of him or simply calling to see if was still alive. Totally amazing how any man could do that to his child. It's just heartless!" Marcy said, "Well, sis, I'm sorry that happened to you, but things will get better." "I know. It just hurts so bad."

Barbra had another idea. "Put his ass on child support. He don't deserve to have a great life with 10 children out there that belong to him, and not even claiming little Keith. Make his ass pay for your baby, Denise." "Barbra, I told Keith I would never take his son from him. I don't believe I should make a man take care of them. That's crazy." Jason said, "Denise, look. If he's not taking care of little Keith, put them people in his life and think nothing about it." "I understand, big brother, but I don't want to make any man take care of his child when he already knows the child has needs." "I'm just saying, sis, too many times these lazy ass men get away with bringing a bunch of kids into the world and the only one who catches all the hell is the mother. It's not fair."

"Brother, thank you for loving me and looking out for me. Keith moved on and changed his work location, which simply means that everything about him has basically been a lie, and actually he's been telling the same lie to every woman he meets. But little Keith and I will be fine." Marcy said, "Denise, honestly, I understand, but you need help, baby." "I am going to make it. I just believe that, sis."

After we talked for another couple of hours, Jason said, "Look sis, it's been a long time, and you need someone in your life. You might remember from several years ago that you met a friend of mine, whose mother lives across the street from your Auntie Mattie Johnson, and I told him about you again. He would like to get to know you better." "I don't know, big brother. With the kids and school, I'm barely making it. I just don't know." "Sis, you need some help." Marcy said, "You might like him."

Jason set up a meeting with his friend, Darren. "Denise, you remember Darren. Darren, you remember my sister Denise." "Denise, how are you doing?" "I'm fine. Thank you for asking." We talked for hours, and eventually Darren asked me out to dinner. He had worked for many years at the U.S. Post Office as a supervisor, and he shared he was looking for a wife--a good one--as he had two children from a former marriage, and the children's mother only came around when it was convenient for her.

The next night, I asked my sister Barbra to baby-sit while I went out on a date with Darren. He drove up in a Cadillac and got out of the door with some beautiful flowers, knocked on the door and gave me a kiss. He then handed me a dozen roses. "Hi. You look beautiful, Denise." "Thank you, Darren. You're looking pretty handsome yourself." "Are you ready to go?" "Yes, I am. Barbra, would you feed the children and put them in bed by 8 p.m.? Otherwise, they'll stay up until 2 or 3 in the morning." I laughed as I told her, "You need your quiet time also." "I got it, sis. Love you and enjoy your night. The kids will be fine, I promise." "I know. Good night."

Darren opened the car door for me, kissed my hand, shut the door and we drove off. "So,

Denise, where do you want to go?" "Surprise me."
"Are you sure?" "Oh, yeah." "Great. Then I will
do just that." Darren took me to the Salt Grass
restaurant, opened the car door for me and then the
restaurant front door. I just smiled and walked in
without saying anything. We were seated
immediately because Darren was known there, and
two wait staff hurried over to our table to take care
of us, because management didn't want him to wait
too long.

"So, Denise, do you know how old I am?"
"No, I don't, but I thought you would tell me."
"I'm nearly fifty years old. Forty-six. How do you
feel about that?" "Yes, you're much older than I
am, but if you can treat me right as you should,
and if being with me is important, then your age
doesn't matter to me." "You're pretty smart for a
young lady." "I've been through a lot in my life,
and I just want a real relationship."

We ended up spending five hours together, then Darren took me back home. It was a couple of weeks before we went out again, and that went well. After that, Darren was coming over to my house every day after he got off work. Two months later, Darren came over to my house. "Denise, how are you?" "I'm fine." "Can we talk?" "Sure. Is something wrong, Darren?" "Yes." "What is it?" "I'm feeling a lot of emotions for you, and I want to be with you every day when I get off work. I know you have three beautiful children, and I will help you with them. I just want to be with you. Denise, please, I've heard of some of your past issues, and I want to take you through that. Can I take you out tonight?" "Yes, Darren, and I like you too." "I know. It's only been six months, but I want to take you to either my house or the hotel of your choice. I want to hold you Denise." "Darren, are you going to be good to me?" We both laughed. "That depends on what you call good, but yes, I'm going to be good to you." "Let me see if my sister Barbra is available, and if she is, I will ask her to keep the kids tonight." "I'll pay her, it's no problem." "Okay, I just asked her and she said yes. I guess I will see you tonight." He said "Yes, you will."

Darren bought me flowers, jewelry and nightwear from Victoria's Secret. He picked me up that night and took me to the Hilton Anatole. We checked into our room, had dinner and went back to our hotel room, where we became intimate. Becoming inseparable, we decided to move in together. Darren, who lived in Arlington, was willing to move to Dallas if I didn't want to move to his house. "Denise, if you want me to move to Dallas, I will let my house go and come here, so we can help each other." "Just for a while, that would be great Darren, but you work in Arlington." "I don't care, as long as I can be with you."

Later, Darren asked me to look into a three-bedroom apartment, and it so happened that there was one available in the complex where I was already living. Darren leased the apartment and gave me a key. I didn't yet recognize that Darren was a very dominating person, and that he needed to have some say, because he already had a plan. However, before I moved out of my place, I let Lenise, Barbra and Jason move in and live there until they were back on their feet.

Chapter Thirty-Two

"I've had enough with you, old broken-down clown. Get away from me." "Bitch, I will kick your ass."

One August day, I started having morning sickness, and I was stressed about it, because the other children were still small. "Darren, I know we didn't totally have a conversation about a child, but I think I'm pregnant." "Really? Well, just make a doctor's appointment and I'll pay to find out."

I made the appointment and we went together. The doctor told me I was three weeks pregnant. "So, she's three weeks pregnant, Doc?" "Yes, and she needs to get some rest." "No problem. Let me know what all is required for her to do and I will make it happen." "Okay. The nurse will bring the discharge papers in, and instructions will be in the release paperwork." "Thanks, Dr. Hope." "Enjoy your day." But I had to say what was on my mind. "I'm having another baby, something I believe I knew before coming here, because I've already had three children. But I'm going to love this one too, Darren. I honestly didn't think I was prepared for more children as I'm on the welfare system, housing, WIC and a 20-hour job, plus struggling to finish school. All without committed help.

"My first two kids' father, whom I'm still married to, beat me until I had to leave and later had other issues, including being locked up. My third child's father was there until the baby was two years old, then he left us to marry his girlfriend after they had been separated for years, and she'd even had another man. Now I'm pregnant with a baby whose father I've only known for almost a year." "Denise, I have two kids already and one more is not going to hurt. That's my kid. Let's just take care of you right now, and when my child comes we will be fine. Stop worrying, okay?" "Okay, Darren. I just want to make sure you're going to take care of your child." "Denise, listen. Nothing in life is a guarantee, but it's a gamble. Sometimes we just have to take a chance on life. I will help you with all the children because I love you, Denise. So, we can stay in the three-bedroom apartment for the year and we will talk again about the next move we make. Okay?" "Okay."

The next nine months went by, and the baby boy was born. "Thank you, Darren, for being at the hospital with me." "Denise, it's my child, too. I needed to come. I'm just sorry I wasn't here when he was born." "He's here now. The nurse will bring him in shortly unless you want to go down to the nursery to see him. We have to name the baby Darren." "Okay, let's do it right now." We decided on Cameron Darren Clark. "I like the name we gave him, Darren." "No, thank you for giving me a son. I will love him and take care of him, no matter what happens to me and you. I will always do my job as a father, Denise."

After three days at the hospital, Darren picked us up, took us home and took care of the baby and me. Of course, he asked my sister Barbra to help when he was at work, which she gladly did, especially because Darren paid her.

Nine months passed, and I noticed that Darren would come home acting differently, being a little more irritated, arrogant and short in conversation, unless it was something he wanted to discuss. This included, for example, his job, how much money he made, the women there who had their own houses and cars, and how many amazing trips they took each year. I wondered often what had brought Darren to this point, but I learned later that as much as he said he hated the ex-wife, he and the children were still doing things together. This is why Darren couldn't get to the hospital in time for the birth of his son, because he couldn't get away from her.

I found out later that Darren hid our relationship from his ex-wife because he didn't know how she would react to the fact that I was a young woman, and that Darren was so much older. One day, Darren came home late, and I had been taking care of the children, so I was extremely tired. Although he left his two kids with me every day when he went to work, and I learned later that he was actually sometimes with his ex-wife. "Darren, where have you been?" "At work. Why?" "What do you mean, why? Because you get off at a certain time and I would like for you to come and check on the house, which includes everyone." "Look, I'm not trying to hear all that. And when you get a job making good money and paying these bills, then I will listen to your ass. In the meantime, shut the hell up with your complaining ass. All you have going for you is the welfare system." "You know what, you bald-headed wanna-be? Get your bad ass kids and get out of my house. I don't need you. All you want is a flunky and a maid to cook your food and take care of your children while you go out dating other women. You have me confused with someone else." "What are you talking about? Because you are the one walking around here mad like something's wrong with your ass." "I've had enough with you, old broken-down clown. Get away from me." "Bitch, I will kick your ass."

Darren hit me a few times, got his kids and left the house. I didn't hear from Darren for a week. During that time, my brother Jason came around and asked, "What happened to you?" "Darren got mad because I asked him where he had been, because I had six kids at the house and I needed help. Plus, I wasn't feeling very well, and he began talking trash and putting me down, and then he hit me, got his two kids and left." "Man, that dude got to deal with me when I ever see his ass. What's wrong with these men, hitting on women? They wouldn't like no other man hitting their Mama, daughter or sister."

Finally, Darren showed up at the apartment complex. Someone recognized his car before he got out, and as soon as he knocked on my door, Jason hit Darren over the head with a stick and then began punching him while his head was bleeding. Jason was angry that this guy had put his hands on me. Darren ran to his car and left.

Three weeks later, Darren called me to check on his baby. "Hi, Denise. How are you and my son?" "I'm fine. Are you okay?" "Yeah, considering I got jumped on. I'm cool. I started to get a gun and shoot your brother." "Well, I'm glad you didn't have one. Can I help you?" "I want my family, Denise, and I want to raise my son. I love you and know I don't act the way I should by you at times. But I love you. Can I come see you tonight without your brother?" "Yes, as long as there won't be any fighting." "I promise there won't be any fighting."

Darren showed up late that night, came into the house and announced that he wanted to be with me for a lifetime. He asked me to move to Arlington and get off welfare for good. He would take care of all the children, put me in a house and buy me a car. Eventually, I gave up my housing, welfare and other benefits for what I thought would be a more normal, middle-class lifestyle, with cars and trips and raising the children together with him. I volunteered at each school and worked at one of the schools as an aide after I graduated from high school in Dallas. I was making clothes for my children and being a great mother to all of them. Darren made sure I had expensive things and some money in my pockets.

One day, I was at work and my children usually went to Dallas over to their grandmother's house, or his children went with their mother when she didn't lie about picking them up. However, on this particular day, I dropped all the children off and told Darren I was going out with my girlfriend. "Denise, go ahead and have a great time. Tonight I'm working late." "Okay, I'll see you in the morning when you get off." "Why don't you spend the night with Leslie Mall, so you won't be home alone?" "You don't mind, Darren?" "No, and I'll come get you when I get up from my nap to take you to eat, unless you just want to come on home." "No, I'll wait. Thanks, baby. I love you. See you in the morning." "I love you, too. See you later."

Later in the evening while at the club with my friend, I started thinking about my conversation with Darren earlier that day. Something about the whole thing didn't feel right. I didn't know that Darren had taken the night off to hang out with friends and women friends. So, I told my friend Leslie that I was going to head to the house. Leslie said, "I thought you were staying at my house tonight." "No, something don't feel right." "What's wrong, Denise?" "I don't know, but I'm about to find out."

I got in my car and made it home to find a strange car sitting in the front of our house, and Darren's car hidden in the garage. Parking down the street and walking carefully back to the house, I made my way to the back of the house where our bedroom was. Darren had the window wide open, while he was having sex with a co-worker. Apparently, he had been dating her for years.

I walked back to the car, got a weapon and went back to the house. I unlocked the door and went in, sparing no thoughts. It was on! And for all the men who had ever hurt me.

Although the godly influence of Mrs. Alice would shine a light on the dark street of my life, drastically changing the direction of my life in later years, that was not on my mind at this particular time.

Read what happened in Volume II

Welcome to My Black Street!

Disclaimer

Dear Readers,

The conversations in *My Black Street: Volume 1* all come from the author's recollections, though they are not written to represent word-for-word transcripts. Rather, Mrs. Grant has retold them in a way that evokes the feeling, and meaning of what was said; still in all instances the essence of the dialogue is accurate. Mrs. Grant has tried to recreate events, locales, and conversations from her memories of them. In order to maintain their anonymity in some instances; Mrs. Grant has changed the names of individuals, places, identifying characteristics, and details such as physical properties, occupations, and places of residence.
Sincerely,

Souls Publishing Distribution & Wholesale

Made in the USA
Middletown, DE
11 April 2023

28543363R00156